The Art of
FLOWER
ARRANGING

SMITHMARK

©Salamander Books Ltd. 1991
129-137 York Way,
London N7 9LG,
United Kingdom

ISBN 0-8317-0423-3

This edition published in 1991 by SMITHMARK Publishers Inc.,
112 Madison Avenue, New York, NY 10016.

SMITHMARK books are available for bulk purchase for sales
promotion and premium use. For details write or telephone
the Manager of Special Sales, SMITHMARK Publishers Inc.,
112 Madison Avenue, New York, NY 10016. (212) 532-6600.

CREDITS

Floral designs by: Jan Hall

Dried flower designs by: Sarah Waterkeyn and John Lewis

Pressed flower designs by: Mary Lawrence

Authors: Angela Vokalek and Coral Walker

Editor-in-chief: Jilly Glassborow

Designers: Kathy Gummer and Barry Savage

Photographers: Steve Tanner

Typeset by: The Old Mill, London

Color separation by: Fotographics Ltd, London – Hong Kong

Printed in Spain

CONTENTS

SECTION ONE

FLOWER ARRANGING

INTRODUCTION

This section takes a fresh, new look at flower arranging,
breaking away from formal designs to create an altogether freer effect.
There are, of course, the more classical designs in conventional vases but, in
the main, the displays are based upon the use of unusual and totally unconventional
containers that can be found in all rooms of the home. Containers such as fancy
paper or plastic bags, toy trucks, goldfish bowls, cake tins, copper kettles,
pineapples and even gumboots! No longer do you need lovely vases
to create stimulating and exotic arrangements.

Apart from step-by-step instructions on how to create the many
beautiful arrangements featured, there is also essential information
on the buying of flowers, how to condition and re-condition them, which
types of foliage to grow at home, the basic equipment and mechanics of flower
arranging, plus the importance of design and colour in creating a well-balanced floral
display. Throughout the book, the plants have been given their most commonly used
name — which is sometimes the Latin name — for example, gypsophila rather than
baby's breath, ivy rather than *Hedera.* For easy reference, a full list of
scientific conversions for this section appears on page 94.

FLOWER ARRANGING

Flower arranging dates back to the ancient Egyptians who used plant material for decorative purposes as long ago as 2,500 BC. Since then other cultures and nations have come and gone, yet the pleasure of decorating our homes with flowers remains. During this century flower arranging has become even more popular and most people have some plant or floral arrangement in their hall or living room.

Flower arranging need not be expensive, especially if you have a garden. As well as background information on how best to prolong the flowers and plants that you display, we have given step-by-step instructions to 120 specific arrangements which can readily be adapted to the availability of flowers and the different types of containers you may have in your home.

BUYING FLOWERS

For many people without a garden, a florist's shop, supermarket or flower stall is the main source of fresh flowers. Although this is more expensive than picking blooms from your own garden, you can ensure you get the best for your money by observing the following guidelines.

Generally, all purchased flowers will need refreshing when they reach your home. Re-cut their stems and give them a long drink for a few hours before transferring them to shallow water and a warm room. Most florists condition flowers before they are sold, so you should only consider re-conditioning them if they begin to wilt (see page 9).

In the spring and summer there will be generally more choice of flowers available. The flowers will probably also be less expensive than in the winter, when most of the florist's stock will either have been imported or grown in hot-house conditions.

Spray chrysanthemums are a good buy all year round as they should last for up to three weeks. During the summer months it is better to buy the outdoor bunch chrysanthemums rather than the more costly forced sprays. When buying these, always look for tight, firm centres and if they are single varieties ensure the centres are firm and yellow as opposed to fluffy and golden.

Spray carnations are another good purchase as they are also good survivors. Buy when they are firm and not fully opened; all the buds should open eventually.

Gladioli are best bought during the summer months, their natural season. Forced, hot-house gladioli can very often not open due to being cut too early.

Orchids are excellent value for money. Both *Dendrobium* and *Cymbidium* orchids can last for as long as two months. Take care when purchasing these flowers though, and avoid buying plants with fully opened sprays or brown-edged petals.

Copper, porcelain, wood, terracotta, plain or coloured glass; traditional, unconventional, modern or antique — all can enhance the natural beauty of flowers.

Stocks are very short-lived, although they are usually inexpensive and emit a beautiful perfume. Their stems quickly become soft and smelly in water, so bear this in mind when arranging.

Freesias — with their powerful fragrance — can live for well over a week if bought when only the first flower is showing, the rest in bud.

All spring bulb flowers should be purchased in bud as their life is short once fully opened.

Roses are best purchased in the summer months when they are in season. In the winter they tend to be expensive and of an inferior quality; consequently they are likely to die without even opening fully.

Most florists' flowers are sold in peak condition, but do seek out a shop where the flowers look healthy and well presented. The golden rule is to look for good, crisp foliage, strong straight stems and tight, firm flower buds.

Although generally more expensive than fresh flowers, dried flowers have the advantage of durability. They are readily available from florists and dried flower specialists, as well as department stores, and come in a wide range of varieties and colours.

EQUIPMENT

A few basic pieces of equipment are necessary before you begin arranging any floral display. These include a good strong pair of florist's scissors or secateurs, a small watering can with a long spout to re-water the arrangement, and a small sharp knife for cutting tough stems or stripping away excess foliage.

Apart from the equipment, actual supports — or mechanics — may also be necessary to arrange the display. Basically, the mechanics are florists' foam, wire mesh or netting, pin-holders and any weighty objects such as marbles, pebbles, shells and so on.

FLORISTS' FOAM
Foam is the most popular mechanic of the florist. It is a specially manufactured substance which readily absorbs water and supports any stems inserted into it, providing they are not too heavy. It can be bought in bricks or rounds of various sizes and, for a fresh arrangement, simply needs soaking in cold water before using. Never let an arrangement in foam dry out as it will not take up water again. Foam meant for fresh displays can be kept moist and sealed in an airtight plastic bag when not used. Foam's only disadvantage is that it tends to break up if the stems are too heavy or if it is over soaked or over used. A form of florists' foam is also available for dried displays.

WIRE MESH
Wire mesh is best for heavy stems and more random fresh displays. It also provides support for many dried flower arrangements. Buy 5cm (2in) mesh, preferably plastic coated, to avoid scratching the inside of your containers. Crumple the mesh and shape it into the container ensuring the holes formed are of an adequate size to receive and support the foliage and flower stems. Important points to remember when using wire mesh are not to crush it too tightly so that it is impossible to insert the stems, and also to leave the mesh more open in the centre where most of the stems will converge.

Equipment and mechanics: 1) Florists' foam for fresh displays; 2) Foam for dried arrangements; 3) Saucers; 4) Plastic pin-holders and 5) Wire U-pins both for securing foam; 6) Fixative; 7) Tape; 8) metal pin-holders for impaling flowers; 9, 10, 11) Cutting implements — scissors and knife; 12) Wire to provide support; 13) Wire mesh; 14) Water spray; 15) Fine-necked watering can with spray.

PIN-HOLDERS
A pin-holder is a heavy metal base studded with a large number of small, upright pins onto which the stems are impaled. A 7.5cm (3in) diameter pin-holder is probably the most useful size for the novice flower arranger. This form of mechanic is particularly useful when designing an arrangement using a limited number of flowers in a shallow container. When introducing the stems to the pin-holder place them vertically and ease them gently to the required angle. Woody stems should be split upwards from the base to help secure them to the pins. Light-weight plastic pin-holders are small devices used, often in conjunction with a fixative, for securing florists' foam to the base of a container.

MARBLES AND PEBBLES
All the above mechanics require to be hidden by the flowers, foliage or the container itself. However, pretty translucent marbles or attractively coloured pebbles provide a form of support which can look particularly impressive when seen through a striking glass container. The stems are inserted into the objects which shift slightly as the arrangement progresses; such mechanics are not therefore ideal for a more regimental display. Other objects, such as shells, can also provide an attractive support for arrangements.

OTHER AIDS
Purpose-designed plastic saucers are useful bases on which to tape florists' foam — dry or soaked — before placing into a container. Apart from tape, U-pins and wire are alternatives for fixing foam to bases, particularly unusual types such as driftwood. Wire is also frequently used in dried flower arranging — either to bind together small bunches of flowers, or to support weak or brittle stemmed plants. Plastic-coated wire is used to support the stems of fragile fresh flowers but should be used sparingly as it can give an unnatural appearance to the plants.

Most living things respond to a little care and attention, and plants are no exception. To prolong the life of cut flowers and foliage you need to condition them (see chart on page 10). Generally, flowers bought from a florist will have been conditioned before they are sold, so they will only need their stems re-cut and a long, cool drink.

It is best to pick flowers from the garden in the early evening when transpiration (water loss) is low and the plant is well charged with 'food' after photosynthesizing all day. Cut the stems at an angle as this allows a larger area to absorb the water. Place immediately into a bucket of tepid water and leave for several hours, even overnight if possible, as this will give the plants time to fully charge up with moisture. Keep in a cool, shady place in summer and a frost-free area in winter. If the place or water is too warm some of the buds may begin to open prematurely. You must also ensure that all plant material is kept away from draughts as these cause dehydration.

Some flowers naturally last longer than others, but all can be prolonged with care. Adding preservatives to the water will help to prolong the life of a display. These can be purchased from a florist or, alternatively, you can simply add a spoonful of sugar, an aspirin tablet or even a dash of lemonade to the water — all work equally well. Before beginning a display, you should also ensure your container is clean as this will help to reduce the growth of stem-clogging bacteria.

All plants take in water through their stems and these vary considerably in structure. Chrysanthemums, stocks and roses have soft, woody stems and such plants need their stem ends crushed lightly with a hammer so that the inner, absorbing, plant tissue is reached. Alternatively, a couple of upward slits can be made in the base of the stem with a sharp knife. Forsythia, rhododendron, lilac and *Prunus* have hard, woody stems. These will need the outside bark scraped off at the base of the stem before crushing or splitting to achieve maximum water absorption.

Soft-stemmed flowers include most spring bulb flowers such as iris, tulips and freesia. These will absorb water quickly and easily so place them in shallow water at first, as deep water may encourage them to open too rapidly. (While conditioning tulips, wrap them in stiff, non absorbent paper for a couple of hours to help them straighten before arranging.) Gladioli — with their strong stems — also need shallow water, but to help all the flowers to open, remove the last few small buds from the tip of the stem to encourage the lower ones to bloom.

Some plants have hollow stems and taller varieties, such as

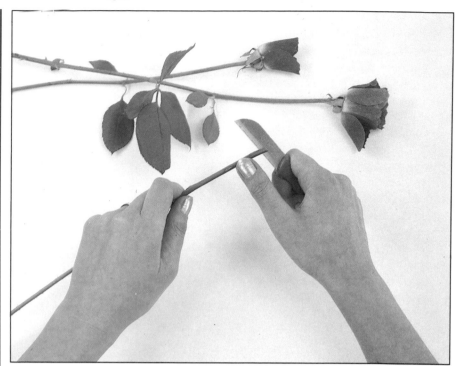

Condition woody stems by making two upward slits with a sharp knife.

delphinium and the larger headed dahlias, require some help to ensure that the water reaches the top of the stem and into the flower head. To do this, turn the bloom upside down, fill up the stem with cold water and plug it with a little cotton wool.

Short-lived flowering shrubs such as lilac, *Viburnum* and mock orange blossom need as much water as possible to reach the flower heads. This can be achieved by stripping off the leaves.

Some flowers are best conditioned through their heads first, rather than their stems. Violets are one such example. Place the heads into tepid water for 30 minutes and then, turning the plants upside down, put the stems into cool, shallow water.

Some plants, such as *Euphorbia* and poppies, emit a milky substance from the cut stem which can form a seal, thus preventing water absorption. To stop this, sear the end of the stem by holding it over a flame until it goes black. (This milky substance can also cause irritation to the skin and should be washed off immediately.)

Straighten and strengthen tulips by wrapping them in non-absorbent paper.

Open out iris flowers prematurely by slicing through sepals with a knife.

Encourage gladioli to open fully by removing last few small buds.

Help woody stems to absorb water by crushing the ends with a hammer.

Sear cut stems by holding over a flame until the end goes black.

RE-CONDITIONING

Generally speaking, it is best to change the water in a display regularly, though some manufacturers of preservatives may recommend that this is not necessary when using their product. Florists' foam in particular needs regular watering to prevent it from drying out; if it does begin to dry out it will cause the flowers to droop. Some flowers, however, may begin to droop even though they have recently been conditioned and are not short of water. In this case the flowers need to be re-conditioned in the following way. Cut off about 2.5cm (1in) from the end of the stems and place them into hot shallow water for ten minutes, protecting the flower heads from the steam with a layer of tissue or soft paper. Then remove the flowers and place them into deep, cool water, leaving them for at least one hour before rearranging them in a display.

FOLIAGE CONDITIONING

A variety of long-lasting foliage is usually obtainable from a florist. Alternatively, there are many attractive varieties that can easily be grown in the garden (see right).

Prolong the life of woody-stemmed foliage such as eucalyptus, rhododendron, camellia, box *(Buxus sempervirens)*, *Ruscus, Cupressus, Pittosporum,* and beech by hammering or slitting their stems before giving them a long drink of water. Ivy and heather like to be totally immersed into deep, cool water for an hour before arranging. Hydrangea heads also like this treatment but for only half the time.

Remember that any foliage placed under the water level in an arrangement will decay, so always strip away any leaves that might otherwise fall beneath the surface of the water.

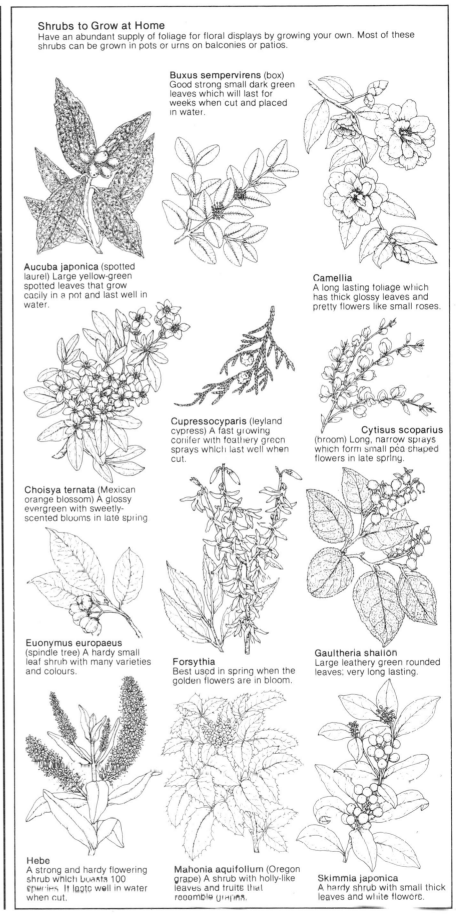

Shrubs to Grow at Home
Have an abundant supply of foliage for floral displays by growing your own. Most of these shrubs can be grown in pots or urns on balconies or patios.

Buxus sempervirens (box) Good strong small dark green leaves which will last for weeks when cut and placed in water.

Aucuba japonica (spotted laurel) Large yellow-green spotted leaves that grow easily in a pot and last well in water.

Camellia A long lasting foliage which has thick glossy leaves and pretty flowers like small roses.

Cupressocyparis (leyland cypress) A fast growing conifer with feathery green sprays which last well when cut.

Cytisus scoparius (broom) Long, narrow sprays which form small pea shaped flowers in late spring.

Choisya ternata (Mexican orange blossom) A glossy evergreen with sweetly-scented blooms in late spring

Euonymus europaeus (spindle tree) A hardy small leaf shrub with many varieties and colours.

Forsythia Best used in spring when the golden flowers are in bloom.

Gaultheria shallon Large leathery green rounded leaves; very long lasting.

Hebe A strong and hardy flowering shrub which boasts 100 species. It lasts well in water when cut.

Mahonia aquifolium (Oregon grape) A shrub with holly-like leaves and fruits that resemble grapes.

Skimmia japonica A hardy shrub with small thick leaves and white flowers.

CONDITIONING CHART

An A-Z of plants and how to treat them

Alstroemeria	Cut stems and place in shallow water.
Amaryllis	Slice off the bottom of stem with a sharp knife. The hollow stem often needs help to support the heavy flower head; when arranging, a thin stick can be gently inserted into the stem.
Anemone	Cut and dip stems in 2.5cm (1in) of boiling water for a few seconds before giving a long drink.
Aster	Crush stem ends and place in 2.5cm (1in) of boiling water before giving an overnight drink.
Bird of paradise	Cut stems on a slant and give a long drink.
Campanula	Cut stems and give a deep drink for a few hours.
Carnation	Cut stems at an angle between joints and place in shallow tepid water.
Christmas rose	Prick stem along its length with a needle and place in deep water.
Chrysanthemum	Cut or crush ends of stems before giving a deep cool drink.
Cornflower	Cut stems and place in water.
Daffodil	See narcissus.
Dahlia	Cut stems and place in water. Wide-stemmed varieties need to be plugged as with delphiniums.
Delphinium	Cut stems. Turn upside down and fill stem with cold water. Plug end with a little cotton wool (cotton).
Forget-me-not	Needs little conditioning except cutting stems and giving a long drink.
Freesia	Cut stems and place in shallow cool water.
Gerbera	Cut stems on a slant and put ends in 2.5cm (1in) of boiling water for a few seconds before giving a long cool drink.
Gladiolus	Cut stems and put in cool, shallow water. Remove the end buds to ensure all flowers will open.
Grape hyacinth	Cut stems and put in cool water.
Gypsophila	Needs little conditioning, except re-cutting stem ends. Easily dried by hanging upside down.
Hyacinth	Cut stems. Then wrap a sheet of non-absorbent paper around flowers and give a long deep drink.
Iris	Cut stems on a slant and give a long drink.
Ixia	Crush stems and place in cool water; if buds are tight, put in 2.5cm (1in) of boiling water for a few minutes first.
Jonquil	See narcissus.
Lilac	Remove all foliage and hammer stems before giving a long drink in warm water.
Lily	Cut stems on a slant or split at base and give a drink in cold water.
Lily-of-the-valley	Garden varieties simply need stems cutting and a drink. Forced ones need stems cutting, wrapping in tissue paper and placing in warm water. They can then be left for several hours completely submerged in cool water before arranging.
Love in a mist	Cut stems and put in water.
Marigold	Cut stems and give a deep drink in cool water.
Mimosa	Immerse the heads in cold water before dipping the stems into 2.5cm (1in) of boiling water for a few seconds. Stand in some warm water until the flowers have dried off.
Narcissus	Cut stems and put in cool, shallow water. Generally, keep daffodils apart from other plants, at least for the first 24 hours, as they produce a poisonous substance which can kill other flowers.
Nerine	Cut stems on a slant before giving a long drink.
Orchid	Generally, orchids last well in water. Cut their stems on a slant and give a long drink. Re-cut stems every few days.
Peony	Cut ends and give a long drink of warm water.
Persian buttercup	Cut and dip stem ends in boiling water before giving a long drink.
Poinsettia	Sear the end of the stem with a flame until it goes black.
Poppy	This needs searing as for the poinsettia.
Primrose	Needs stems cutting and placing in water.
Protea	Hammer the ends before giving a long drink.
Pyrethrum	These last well as cut flowers and simply need their stems re-cut before being given a long drink.
Rose	Crush the ends of florists' roses before giving a long drink in warm water. Roses from the garden need their stems placed in boiling water for about a minute before being given a long drink. Roses can be revived with an aspirin tablet or a teaspoonful of sugar.
Scabious	Cut the ends of the stems and give a long, overnight drink.
Snapdragon	Cut stems and give a long deep drink for an hour or so. Forced blooms need a few seconds with their stems in 2.5cm (1in) of boiling water first.
Snowdrop	Cut stems and place in bunches in a little cool water.
Stock	Hammer stem ends and remove all foliage below the water line before giving a long drink.
Sweet pea	Trim stem ends and place in deep water in a cool place. Handle as little as possible.
Sweet william	Cut stems and give a long drink.
Trollius	Cut and dip stem ends into boiling water, then give a deep drink of cool water.
Tulip	Cut stems and wrap flowers in stiff, non-absorbent paper for a couple of hours to strengthen and straighten them. Place in shallow water. Tulips also like a little aspirin.
Violet	Place the flower heads upside down in tepid water for 30 minutes and then reverse, cut stems and place the stems into cool shallow water.
Zinnia	These hollow stems need to be cut and given a long drink. Provide a little support with a thin piece of coated wire inserted into the stem if it is especially fragile.

Flower arranging is a decorative art form and, as with any other artform, you must appreciate the colour, texture and proportions of your materials in order to create a pleasing, well-balanced design. The best of flowers and foliage can look positively 'wrong' if too little thought has been given to putting the various elements together. Always remember that time spent planning your design before you actually begin an arrangement is never time wasted.

First consider the colours in your display. Do you wish to create total harmony, choosing colours from the same area of the colour spectrum as in Pink on Parade on page 12? Or do you want to use brightly contrasting colours for a more striking effect, as in Floral Confection on page 82? The colour wheel on the right shows how the various colours of the spectrum relate to each other — colours on opposite sides of the wheel are contrasting, adjacent colours are toning. White is also an important factor in any design as it can be used to create highlights. Similarly, dark colours, particularly dark foliage or deeply coloured flowers, add depth to an arrangement.

Look at the different textures of your materials and consider how they could be used to add interest to your display. Materials such as grasses, foliage, twigs, coral, cones, poppy seed heads or unusual flowers such as sea lavender, safflowers or bells of Ireland provide a contrast of texture that can be used to great effect.

The proportions of your flowers and foliage will largely dictate the position of the various plants within the display. Tall plants are usually used to establish the height or outline of a display, while bold flowers or full blooms often form the focal point, or centre, of an arrangement. Other less prominent flowers and foliage are used to fill in the outline. Fine, wispy flowers such as gypsophila (baby's breath) can be used to break up the outline.

Before you begin, you should decide on the general shape of your arrangement: whether it is to be symmetrical or asymmetrical, triangular or semi-circular. Also, do you wish to create a traditional design or a more free-flowing and random one? Above all, whichever type you choose to create, you must ensure that your display is well-balanced, looking neither top heavy nor lopsided.

Finally, you should give some thought to the setting of your arrangement. Be sure to keep your display in proportion to your vase or container. Consider also where you will place the display within a room and the angle from which it is to be viewed. Whether the display is to be seen from side-on, above or all sides will effect the shape of your

This wheel is a guide to colour harmony. Warm colours (red, yellow, orange) sit on one side of the wheel, the cool colours (blue, violet, green) on the other. Contrasting colours are those opposite each other on the wheel.

arrangement. You may also wish to reflect the colour scheme of your room or your vase in your choice of flowers. Lighting is also important. Natural light is ideal for showing off a display to its best advantage, but if you need to use artificial light, make sure it is shone from above rather than below; if you light a display from below you will lose most of the colour values and the arrangement will look flat.

Right: Flowers and foliage placed equally on each side of an arrangement form a symmetrical display.

Centre: Long stems have been used to create a strong diagonal line running through this attractive asymmetrical arrangement.

Far right: Flowers are clustered into groups in a continental fashion in this triangular arrangement.

Symmetrical

Asymmetrical

Triangular

The frosty pink glass of this art deco vase is reflected in the flowers of the display. Squash up a piece of wire mesh and squeeze into the bottom of the vase: the mesh will be masked by the frosted glass. Add long stems of pink broom to form the curving outline. Then fill in the outline with pink miniature roses.

Pink gerbera form the focal point. Place one above the other to the front of the arrangement, with three more looking out from the sides. Finally, fill in the gaps with pinks, recessing some of the flowers as shown to create depth in the arrangement.

The beauty of these 'triangular'-shaped vases is that they can be used to create an attractive 'sweeping fan' effect. Place marbles in the vase to stabilize the arrangement before adding water. Then begin the outline with yellow broom, curving the pieces out from the vase.

Arrange the remaining flowers in groups. First, the yellow lilies, keeping the flowers at differing heights to obtain maximum focal effect; next the white chrysanthemums on the opposite side.

Fill in the outline with stems of *Oncidium ornithorhynchum* orchids and a spray of forsythia.

The bold yellows and reds of the flowers offset the deep blue glass of this attractive 1930s bowl. Crushed wire mesh is the best medium for this type of shallow bowl as it keeps the flowers from sagging.

A silver rose bowl is designed to show off roses to their best advantage as this rich display of full blown yellow roses and golden freesias demonstrates. Fill the bowl with water. Then cut short the stems of the cream spider chrysanthemums (to around 5cm, 2in) and pack into the bowl's wire mesh centre — these will give depth to the final arrangement.

Place yellow roses in between the chrysanthemums, keeping the stems slightly longer. Next, intersperse the arrangement with a few freesias.

Finally, place *Leucodendron* and freesia buds among the display, ensuring the stems are slightly longer than those of the other flowers; these will provide a stark contrast to the gold and silver. For a short period of time, such as during a dinner party, a full blown rose at the foot of the bowl will complete the picture, though, out of the water, the bloom's lifespan will be limited.

Fill mesh with variegated *Pittosporum,* a bushy foliage which maintains its fullness even when cut short. Stems of gypsophila (also known as baby's breath in the United States) are added next, spread across the arrangement.

The three main stems of yellow lily, straddling the length of the vase, form the focal point. Intersperse the whole display with holly (known more specifically as English holly in the United States) berries, retaining the longer twigs for contrast and balance.

A mass of flowers in harmonizing blues, lilacs, purples and white combine to create a splendid arrangement, ideal for an entrance hall or lobby. Pack soaked florists' foam into the neck of a plain glazed pot. Begin with the tallest flowers first: purple statice and blue dyed yarrow. Work in descending stages so that each flower is 'sitting' on another.

Working gradually downwards, intermix the statice and yarrow with white daisy chrysanthemums, delphiniums and *Euphorbia marginata,* having seared this latter plant first (see page 8). Keep some of the upper leaves on the stems of the flowers as these give depth to the display. To finish, follow through the shape of the arrangement with blue-dyed carnations.

Brighten up a potted plant with a few added flowers. Insert several little phials — or any small, slim containers — of water into the soil of the plant. Place them evenly around the pot and fill with long stems of mimosa so that the flowers occupy the spaces between the leaves. Mimosa works very well with this dumb cane, picking up the yellow-green of the variegated leaves.

Complete the effect by placing the pot into a pottery plant holder. This display should last well, but remember to water the phials regularly. An equally pleasing effect can be achieved using just one or two small containers of water, placed at the back or side of the display, and filled with a small group of flowers.

An old water jug and bowl provide a perfect setting for this traditional mass arrangement, with its bold contours and colours. Wedge left-over scraps of soaked florists' foam into the jug. Then position a few large stems of bells of Ireland with two or three garlic flowerheads to establish the height and outline.

Place white statice and grey *Kochia* (summer cypress) foliage to fill in the outline, keeping the stems around 5cm (2in) shorter than the garlic and bells of Ireland. Next add scabious (known as pincushion flower in the United States) among the statice and *Kochia*. Already the colours complement the jug and bowl beautifully.

Brilliant red Persian buttercups, placed within the mass, instantly lift the arrangement, their colour and texture a striking contrast to the existing plants. To finish, place a small sprig of lacey *Viburnum tinus* inside the bowl to the fore of the jug, or, instead, more short-stemmed flowers can be added to the bowl, surrounding the jug.

Here, a rich and traditional display has been created using a wide range of varieties and colours. A vase such as this needs only water, but crushed wire mesh or florists' foam can be used. Begin by filling the jug with variegated *Pittosporum* — this will give the arrangement depth. Then intersperse a few spider chrysanthemums for contrasting texture.

On this solid base add a good mixture of flowers to develop a symmetrical display. The arrangement shown here uses mainly carnations, chrysanthemums, gerbera and scarlet tobacco plant (known as flowering tobacco in the United States) in co-ordinating colours.

This traditionally shaped vase looks particularly attractive with a bright and bold symmetrical arrangement. The blues reflect the vase while the pink of the gerbera is a perfect complement and forms the focal point of the display. Fill the vase with water and build up the outline using eucalyptus and September flowers (a form of aster).

Curve the eucalyptus down towards the base of the display, and position the feathery September flowers upright at the back. Add to the outline by inserting a few stems of pink gladioli, one shorter than the others. (Tip: nip out the 'plait' at the end of the gladiola stem before arranging as this encourages the buds to open and makes the display last longer.)

Simplicity itself, this modern design relies on straight lines and bold colours to create a striking effect. Carefully fill an oblong glass vase with marbles, then cover with water.

Cut three stems of amaryllis — two of similar length and one slighty longer — and push into the marbles. The hollow amaryllis stems will curl when placed into water, so the marbles are excellent for holding them in position.

Position the two shorter stems together on one side of the vase, the other longer one on the opposite side.

Fill in the outline with white and blue delphiniums. Then add the focal flowers by positioning five or six stems of gerbera at the front of the arrangement. Recess a few white spray chrysanthemums and finish off with two or three stems of bells of Ireland to contrast with the soft texture of the other flowers.

Adeep blue vase in art nouveau style is cleverly contrasted by an exquisite arrangement of gentle colours and contours. Put only water into the vase; the vase's tight neck will support the display. Position several sprays of sprengeri fern, curving one piece so that it sweeps down in front of the vase. Then two long stems and one shorter one of pale creamy-pink alstroemeria.

Create a central column using white lilac; this will give depth to the arrangement. Then take stems of pink daisy chrysanthemums in graduating lengths and place throughout the display.

This stunning display of rich pinks and purples beautifully complements the handsome lilac-glazed vase. Using a tall vase, such as this, warrants a lofty arrangement. Begin by putting some chunks of soaked florists' foam into the vase and creating the outline with long stems of eucalyptus. Strengthen the outline with four or five deep pink gladioli.

Cut dark purple spray chrysanthemums to varying lengths and form a 'central column' through the middle of the display, leaving one small flower head to hang gently down over the rim of the vase. Follow this line with four deep pink roses. Finally, use delicate sprays of *Dendrobium* orchids to strengthen the outline, reserving one or two to gently curve downwards.

In this attractive arrangement, gently flowing lines and contours have been created with just three varieties of flower. And the salt jar — with its 'open mouth' — provides a perfect backdrop, with both the top and the base clearly visible in the completed display. First, place a piece of soaked florists' foam into the jar.

Begin the display with several stems of delphinium. Their naturally curving stems will form a gentle outline. Recess a little bouvardia into the jar to create depth.

The central flowers are alstroemeria. Push most of them well into the centre, leaving several longer stems to protrude and strengthen the outline.

This beautiful arrangement is worthy of a wedding reception, and it's not too difficult for an amateur flower arranger. First place a block of florists' foam in the centre of a large salver. Make a 'skirt' around the edge by sticking laurel leaves horizontally into the base of the foam. Add some eucalyptus sprays to build up the shape.

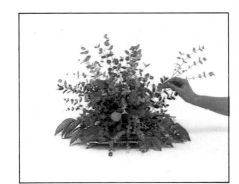

When you have created a triangular shape, add sprays of white gladioli and arum lilies (also known as calla lily) to contrast with the greenery. In placing these, aim for a balanced effect, beginning with a lily in the centre and working out and around. Remember that if the arrangement is to be seen from all sides, you must keep turning it to check for gaps.

Next, insert sprays of chrysanthemum and white lilac among the other white flowers. Keep checking all sides of the arrangement to maintain the balance.

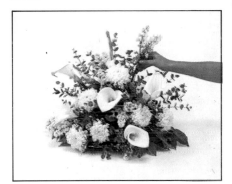

The final colour contrast is provided by tulips and roses in varying shades of pink. Here again it is important to maintain symmetry, so work around the arrangement, filling in where colour is lacking. Allow some of the blooms to lie over the edge of the salver by pushing their stalks horizontally into the foam.

The kitchen is often the first place to look for useful containers. Pretty aluminium cases such as these are shiny and create attractive highlights. Place a piece of soaked florists' foam into the case. Then add long stems of *Viburnum tinus* to create the outline.

A shallow ovenware dish forms the base for this arrangement of fiery chrysanthemums, carnations and capsicums (also known as Christmas pepper in the United States). Place soaked florists' foam into the dish and cover with *Viburnum tinus* allowing the stems to escape over the sides of the dish.

To create the focal point of the arrangement, take six full blooming orange carnations and arrange them uniformly across the outline.

Spray some longer stems of eucalyptus with silver paint and, when they are dry, slot them in among the *Viburnum*. Paint-sprayed dried foliage is an excellent addition to any arrangement especially when using a metallic base or container.

Form the focal point of the display, and help to fill in the outline, using dark red spray carnations — both buds and full flowers. For depth, recess some dark red *Viburnum* buds. A little water and a few flowers in the mini cases complete the display.

Fill in the outline with greenish white spray chrysanthemums. Their colour provides a dramatic contrast to the orange carnations, and their flame-shaped petals aptly fit the theme of the arrangement. Complete the display with capsicums, taking them through and along the length of the arrangement.

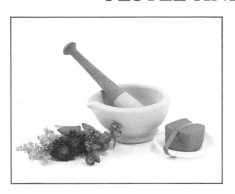

Astoneware pestle and mortar forms an unusual and attractive setting for an arrangement, the soft neutral colours complemented by the grey-green foliage and strikingly contrasted by the rich pinks and purples. To begin, tape soaked florists' foam to a small dish which will fit inside the mortar.

Build up the outline of the arrangement with the grey succulent foliage *Kochia* (summer cypress) — this will give depth to the final display. Add a few blue-purple forget-me-nots, placing them among the foliage.

Position dark pink spray chrysanthemums to form the focal point of the arrangement and to help fill in the outline. Finally add some stems of striking *Mallalika* foliage. To create an asymmetrical effect place the *Mallalika* so that it flows diagonally (as shown here). Follow this line with some long stems of chrysanthemum buds.

This stunning display resembles a rather spectacular hat and is easily created using a plain round cake tin. Tape a piece of soaked florists' foam on to a saucer and place inside the tin. Create the outline with variegated and ordinary *Ruscus* and white snapdragons, using the latter to form a gentle diagonal line.

The main focal flowers are deep red chrysanthemums — graduate their height so they completely fill the centre of the display. To finish the arrangement take six or seven stems of red *Arachnis* (scorpion) orchids and position them throughout the display, strengthening and extending the outline.

Create a pretty country picture with a wicker bread basket and a selection of colourful garden flowers. Tape a piece of soaked florists' foam into a small saucer and place in the basket. Cover the foam with *Viburnum tinus* foliage, then take long, feathery stems of yellow broom and position so that a 'spidery' effect is formed.

Add bolder yellow flowers in the form of clumps of forsythia, cut quite short and rising up from the centre and towards the foreground of the display.

Create the focal point using rust-coloured daisy chrysanthemums to form a dome shape, and fill in any gaps with a few sprays of golden freesias.

A fondue sitting on a burner acts rather like a vase on a pedestal, with both the flowers and the container easily visible — as the bright orange of the pan is an integral part of the display this is quite important. First, put a large piece of soaked florists' foam into the pan. Then form the outline with feathery foliage such as *Mallalika*.

Fill in the centre of the display with peach coloured spray chrysanthemums. Take longer stems of dark red *Arachnis* (scorpion) orchids and place them sparingly throughout the arrangement, following and strengthening the basic outline.

Five red roses form the focal point and balance the colour of the display. Keep four roses of much the same height in the centre, with one longer stem rising from the back and curving gently outwards.

This low circular arrangement could serve well as a centrepiece on a large round table. Tape soaked florists' foam to a dinner plate and place in the basket. Cover the foam with partly-sprayed gold hydrangea heads. Then position six or seven open lilies and two or three buds amidst the hydrangea, keeping the stems short so that they sit low.

Add deep rust spray chrysanthemums — cut even shorter — to nestle close in behind the lilies, giving depth. Contrast these with paler coppery spider chrysanthemums, inserting them in any gaps. To finish, dot longer stems of brown preserved eucalyptus and pieces of coral sparingly throughout the arrangement. These give contrast both in colour and texture.

Arusset-coloured terracotta chicken brick or casserole provides a perfect setting for an orange and golden arrangement. Place a large piece of soaked florists' foam into the 'dish' of the chicken brick. Begin the display with feathery *Mallalika* foliage, fanning it out at the back to establish the height and positioning several stems forward to give a base for the flowers.

Recess a few pale yellow spidery chrysanthemums. Now take several longer stems, place two or three to the right of the arrangement and position two slightly shorter ones on the left, so that they sit on the rim of the dish. Add several rust-coloured daisy chrysanthemums, spreading them throughout the display.

Fill out the arrangement with deep orange carnations, bringing one slightly forward over the rim of the dish. Balance this with a corresponding tall carnation at the back. Complete the display with long stems of yellow broom, following the outline of the *Mallalika*.

Add some water to the lid of the chicken brick and position a few stems of foliage and a flower or two. Keep the plants lying low so that they enhance, and do not detract, from the main display.

Brilliant scarlet anemones dominate this lovely display which nestles in an old-fashioned enamelled colander. Tape a piece of soaked florists' foam to a saucer and secure it in the colander with some florists' fixative. Then use feathery marguerite foliage to cover the foam and form the base and outline for the flowers.

This is a rather enterprising use for an ordinary metal sieve, and one which works surprisingly well with wintery flowers and foliage. Use a piece of soaked florists' foam wrapped completely in cling film (plastic wrap) as the base for the sieve. Adhere the sieve to the foam with some wire or pins. Next secure another soaked brick of foam inside the sieve.

The final effect is one of a 'ball' of flowers sitting on a stand. This rounded effect is created with the red anemone flowers which should be positioned with their faces looking up and out from the display.

Cover the foam with flowering *Viburnum tinus*, creating both a solid base for the display and a strong diagonal line. This will give the eye a firm visual route to follow.

Now the outline has been created with the flowers and foliage, fill in the gaps with sprays of pretty September flowers (a form of aster). These contrast well in both texture and colour, and enhance the focal flowers — the anemones.

Take the very palest of pink spray chrysanthemums, cutting the individual flowers from the sprays rather than using the main stem. Position a few full flowers in the centre of the display to form the focal point. Several longer stems of chrysanthemum buds and flowers can then be interspersed throughout the outline.

This beautiful Doulton cheese dish is enhanced by a mass of russets and creams and would make a striking centrepiece at a dinner party.

The bright red label and seal of an old-fashioned mustard jar has been cleverly picked up by the scarlet carnations. To begin the display, put a piece of soaked florists' foam into the mustard jar.

Fix some soaked florists' foam to a pin-holder placed in the centre of the base. Use short stems of rust coloured chrysanthemums to establish the outline of the display. Place the tallest chrysanthemum in the centre; the rest should graduate down to the shortest stems near the base.

Fill the jar with carnation foliage and intersperse with red carnation buds and flowers. Offset the rather symmetrical look by creating a diagonal line with a few stems of variegated ivy.

Between the chrysanthemums insert cream spray carnations, recessing them into the arrangement. Rust-dyed sea lavender should be used to fill in any gaps and a few trailing stems will serve to balance the display.

A Chinese wok and rice bowl form an unusual but effective setting. Tape soaked florists' foam to a shallow dish and place inside the wok. Position four exotic bird of paradise leaves to create a sweeping line and add a few bird of paradise flowers. Use *Leucodendron* foliage to cover any visible foam and trail some over the wok edge.

Varying lengths of yellow spider chrysanthemums help form the centre of the arrangement: keep the long stems to the back and shorter stems to the fore. Position capsicum (known as Christmas pepper in the United States) stems throughout the arrangement to form the focal point. The capsicums will also pick up the red of the bird of paradise.

Delicate *Oncidium ornithorhynchum* orchids soften the effect of the arrangement: position two or three stems to take up the sweeping line of the bird of paradise leaves. Then add the bear grass, curving it up above the arrangement to create the 'oriental' effect.

Insert a few remaining flowers into some soaked florists' foam in the small rice bowl. Keep the stems short except for a longer spray or two of *Oncidium* orchid which reflect the main arrangement.

With its contrasting colours and textures, this attractive display is a mass of flowers, foliage and wood. Two cast iron skillets, set with soaked florists' foam, form the basis of the display. Begin with the larger skillet, covering the foam with *Choisya ternata* foliage to create an outline. Slot several orange tulips among the outline, curving one tulip down beyond the pan handle.

Recess some stems of peach coloured *Euphorbia fulgens* in among the tulips and foliage, reserving two or three stems to rise up at the side and back of the display. (Remember to sear the *Euphorbia* first, see page 8). The smaller skillet contains a very simple arrangement of Portuguese laurel leaves and white lilies. Use just three lilies, cutting them short so that they nestle among the foliage.

Brass provides good highlights for floral displays and while not as warm as copper is an excellent foil for these pale autumn colours. This brass French chocolate pot is especially pretty with its wooden handle. Cut a deep piece of florists' foam to fit into the pot and soak it well.

A salt box can serve as an unusual wall-vase, and this copper one provides a beautiful burnished setting for the reds and peachy colours of the flowers and foliage. First, place florists' foam into the salt box and prop open the lid at an interesting angle using a stem, twig or piece of wire.

Use about eight dried onion heads to create the outline, placing the tallest two first to establish the height and then adding progressively shorter ones on either side to form a dome-shaped outline. Mixing dried and fresh flowers can be very effective, but be sure to use wet florists' foam!

Create a gentle diagonal line with preserved eucalyptus stems and follow this line with pale peach spray carnations, keeping the stems slightly shorter than the eucalyptus and in varying lengths. The two contrast beautifully. Recess a couple of carnations into the display to give depth and the impression that the flowers are bursting out.

Next, take peach spray carnations of similar graduating heights and slot them in between the onion heads, filling in the outline. Finally, to complete the main arrangement, coral can be used to add a contrast of texture and help give substance. A strategically placed piece of coral and a carnation head lying with the lid complete the picture.

Finally, place one orange lily in the centre to serve as the focal point. Two or three lily buds positioned close to the centre will open subsequently and add further interest and colour to the display.

The plants in this dried flower arrangement have been specially chosen to blend with the rusty tones of the terracotta pot. Start by packing wire mesh into the base of the pot, leaving about 1cm (½in) protruding from the top. Put the lid at a rakish angle over two-thirds of the pot, making sure it is well balanced.

Wire small bunches of South African daisy (a form of helichrysum) and push them into the mesh. Next add wired bunches of peachy cluster-flowered sunray, filling in the arrangement.

Finally, add stems of pink-dyed *Leucodendron brunia* throughout, pushing some deep into the arrangement, keeping others long so that the bobbly heads break through the outline and hang over the sides of the pot.

A stoneware hot water bottle holds a pretty display of dried flowers. Begin by slicing a sphere of florists' foam in half and gouging out the centre of one piece with a knife. Push this foam over the opening of the bottle so that it fits snugly and is held firmly in place. Now wire several bunches of daisy-like rhodanthe (sunray) and insert them into the foam.

Once you have formed the outline, fill the centre of the display with three dryandra; push them deep down in amongst the rhodanthe. Finish off with a few wired groups of bright yellow yarrow to add a splash of colour.

In the centre add some sprays of honesty (silver dollar plant); its silvery heads will lighten the solid mass of mustards and browns. Brown-dyed teasels can be added next — their spiky heads peeking out from the other plants, providing contrasting texture and complementary colour. Against these muted colours dot a sprinkling of bright mixed helichrysum.

An old wicker shopping basket provides an excellent setting for a long-lasting dried arrangement. Take a whole brick of florists' foam and fix to a pin-holder in the base of the basket. Disguise the foam by packing pieces of beige-dyed sea lavender all around it and inserting natural sea lavender into the centre.

Fill in with yellow-dried flowers — lady's mantle and golden rod — allowing some longer stems to trail over the edge of the basket. Lengthen the whole arrangement with stems of bells of Ireland, creating a long diagonal line across the length of the basket. Follow this line with brown grasses.

Finally, complete with some preserved beech leaves. (Preserve in advance by mixing one part glycerine to two parts hot water. Give beech stems a good drink of water first then place into the solution and leave for about 10 days, coating the leaves with a little of the mixture. Store in a box until ready to use.)

Here, an oblong pie dish forms the base of another low and oriental-style arrangement, in which flowers and foliage are used to create a miniature garden. Put left over chunks of soaked florists' foam into a pie dish and cover with bun moss.

Popular in Japan, displays such as this are designed to look like miniature gardens. Here, a round pie dish has been used to form the shallow base. Begin by putting slices of soaked florists' foam of varying thickness into the bottom of the dish and cover with bun moss.

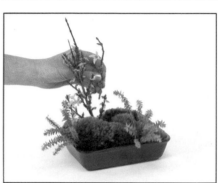

Insert a little *Leucodendron* foliage and two or three sprays of forsythia to serve as trees and bushes.

Then take two or three different types of foliage in graduating heights (shown here is *Leucodendron*) and position among the moss mounds.

Then add a small cluster of miniature carnations and *Viburnum tinus* flowers to the foreground, serving as the flowers of the garden and forming the focal point of the display.

Cluster some alstroemeria to the foreground, keeping them low and 'bushy'. Place a little *Viburnum tinus* at each side of the alstroemeria. Cut down a gladiolus and insert at an angle so that it sits like a ship's masthead on the rim of the dish. Complete with a few miniature carnations, in the same colour as the gladiolus, rising up and meeting the foliage behind.

This is a good way of using up broken flower heads or those flowers which could last a few days longer if cut short. Stick double-sided tape around the outside edge of a sponge ring mould. Adhere pleated green cellophane to this and secure with a little more sticky tape. This creates an attractive trim and is an alternative to foliage.

. . . and all things nice! An unused spice rack makes a promising wall vase. Use only a few of the jars available, otherwise the arrangement will look too crowded. Fill the jars with water and begin from the left with a small cluster of deep purple anemones and pink roses. Use about six flowers in all. Then move on to another jar.

Insert chunks of soaked florists' foam into the ring, placing slightly thicker pieces at the back. Working around the ring insert short stems of daisy chrysanthemums to complete the circle.

In a second jar place another dark purple anemone and some pale pink alstroemeria. Finally, create a tall arrangement at the end with dark pink roses, white stock and matching pink tulips. The stock is quite a tall flower, so establish the height with this before cutting any of the other flower stems too short.

Throughout the chrysanthemums dot blue-dyed yarrow and some little gold-sprayed cones on wires. Three white candles complete the garland. (The non-drip variety are best for a floral arrangement.)

Using this unusual plant pot holder, three individual arrangements combine to form an attractive display. Place soaked florists' foam into each pot and then arrange the pots one at a time. Fill the first with two lengths of delphiniums, the open flowers close to the rim of the pot, the longer stems sweeping out. Among this recess clumps of *Viburnum tinus.*

In the second pot place six or seven open pinks and two or three buds. Recess with pretty September flowers (a form of aster) to add depth to the arrangement.

The third pot forms the focal point of the whole arrangement, with purple and lilac anemones looking up and out, interspersed with tiny pink carnation flowers and leaves. Allow a trail of ivy to wend its way from the saucer at the base of the pots to complete the display.

The warm, earthy quality of terracotta is often used to house plants. Here, three small, plain little pots set off the different types of fresh flowers beautifully. Soaked florists' foam can be used for the larger two pots, water only for the small one. Start by arranging several anemones in the largest pot.

Position three pink hyacinths of graduating lengths in the medium bowl. Fill in around the base with *L. brunia,* leaving the feathery foliage trailing over the edge. To finish, fill the small bowl with short stems of white daisy chrysanthemums.

Add longer stems of pink broom, setting it at a rakish angle on each side. To fill in the outline use longer stemmed Persian buttercup buds. Depth and contrasting texture is provided with two stems of *Leucodendron brunia.* Recess one deep into the pot, the other longer piece towards the back.

An old stoneware hot water bottle and kitchen jar make a simple but effective display when placed together. Use crushed wire mesh to hold the arrangement in the jar and position the yellow gerbera to form a gentle contour.

Take longer stems of *Oncidium ornithorhynchum* orchids, and fill in behind and around the gerbera, following the contour already established. A finger of foam inserted into the hot water bottle will take the smaller arrangement. This comprises a stem of gerbera cut short and a sprig of *Oncidium*.

COFFEE TIME

PIG IN PINK

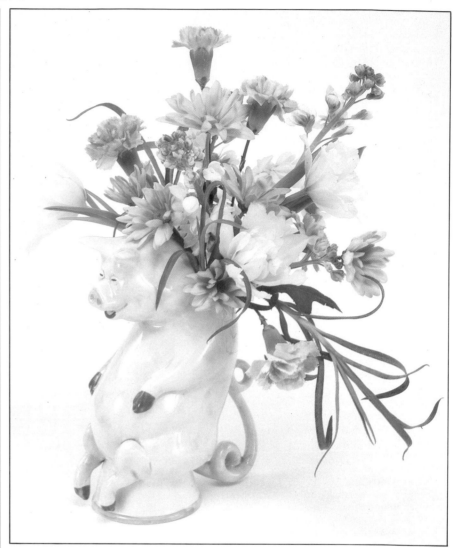

Astriking red enamel coffee pot and mug form the basis for this pretty display of red anemones. Place some soaked florists' foam into the coffee pot and fill with clumps of flowering marguerite foliage.

Among the marguerite foliage slot three or four pieces of seared *Euphorbia marginata* (see page 8). Fill in this outline with graduating heights of bright red anemones, reserving three longer stems to serve as a 'spout'.

The smaller arrangement is created quickly and easily. Take a piece of soaked florists' foam, place it in the mug and fill it with the remaining clumps of marguerites.

When using novelty containers such as this, try to keep flowers and foliage to a minimum so that both plants and container can be fully enjoyed. Put a piece of soaked florists' foam into the jug and build up the outline with a few flowers. In this case, the pig's soft shades have been picked out with pink-edged white double tulips and white stock.

To fill out the display add longer stems of pale pink spray carnations and pink daisy chrysanthemums. Extra length and contrast can be achieved with two or three carnation leaves.

Aquaint cottage tea-pot serves as an excellent vase, with the colours of the cottage picked-out by the clever choice of flowers. Begin by placing some soaked florists' foam into the teapot and insert stems of eucalyptus to form a base for the display.

Next, add four or five pink-edged white double tulips, placing the longest tulip stem in the centre of the arrangement to establish the height. Keep the tulip leaves on the stems as their texture and colour add contrast to the other flowers and foliage.

Fill in the outline with purple-dyed sea lavender, recessing some pieces to create depth. Finally, take a few purple anemones and position them throughout the display. As the focal flowers of the display their faces should be prominent.

Once again a tea-pot has been employed as a flower holder. This pot — in the shape of an elephant — is a little more novel than most, but the idea can be adapted to suit any type of pot. Put a crushed piece of wire mesh into the tea-pot and add some water.

Enhance the lovely grey colour of the pot by using similar coloured foliage. Shown here is small leafed eucalyptus 'sprinkled' with gypsophila (also known as baby's breath in the United States). This creates the basic outline of the arrangement.

Use dramatic lilac and purple anemones to create the focal point, forming an 'umbrella' over the foliage. The darker anemones also give the display depth and a velvety texture. Fill in the outline with pink miniature carnations.

An obsolete electric copper kettle, burnished and glowing, makes an attractive and practical container for flowers. Remove the lid, which can be used as an accessory to the arrangement, and place a piece of soaked florists' foam into the kettle.

Take three pieces of eucalyptus and arrange to create a 'triangle' which sweeps down diagonally to the base of the kettle. Next, recess some dark rust chrysanthemums among the foliage, allowing a few longer stems to protrude. Finally, use three or four orange lilies to add colour and to form the focal point, placing their 'faces' to look forward from the centre of the display.

The glow of polished copper provides a perfect setting for this contrasting warm auburn and pale yellow arrangement. Cut and soak half a block of florists' foam and place it in the base of a saucepan. Then form the outline using *Leucodendron.* The larger stem seen here — *L. bruniu* — has an interesting texture and helps create depth in the arrangement.

Using a combination of buds and fully opened flowers, take the yellow carnations and arrange them at random around and among the *Leucodendron.*

Next, insert the coppery spider chrysanthemums around the base of the arrangement and towards the top. Then add longer stems of preserved eucalyptus to form a gentle diagonal line pointing down towards the smaller saucepan. To complete the arrangement, fill the second pan with yellow spider chrysanthemums — a simple effect which enhances the main arrangement.

A battered old shovel that has seen better days makes a novel setting for this brightly coloured display. Begin by cutting a section from a cylinder of florists' foam and taping it on to the base of the shovel. Form an outline using stems of golden rod then fill in with yarrow, positioning the latter deeper down in the arrangement to cover the foam.

To contrast the bright yellow of the yarrow, dot some dark oak leaves throughout the display. Then form a ring of leaves around the base. Add highlights with a few clumps of creamy helichrysum (strawflower or everlasting).

An old iron that hasn't seen a board for many a day is given a second lease of life as part of an imaginative dried arrangement. Cut a slice off a cylinder of florists' foam and attach it to the iron with a narrow strip of florists' tape. Begin to build up the shape of the display using wired clumps of lady's mantle.

Finally, bring the arrangement fully alive with several groups of Chinese lantern. Push them deep down so that they peep out from amongst the other plants.

Next, add small bunches of blue larkspur, evenly dotted throughout the arrangement. Follow with clumps of pink miniature sunray, pushing some of them deep into the display.

To finish, add clumps of bold yellow button chrysanthemums, putting them mainly around the edges of the arrangement, and using them to fill in any gaps, and cover any tape still exposed.

An old flour sieve provides a frame for this pretty dried flower design. Cut a sphere of florists' foam in two and tape one half on to the side of the sieve. Build up a spiky outline using ears of wheat, pushing them singly into the foam. Keep the arrangement asymmetrical by making the stems longer on one side so that they spill out of the bottom of the 'frame'.

Follow the general outline already created using pink larkspur, keeping it as tall as the wheat. Intersperse the arrangement with South African daisies (a type of helichrysum). Place them at varying heights, then add depth with several bunches of moon grass, pushing them well into the display.

Complete the picture with a small posy on top of the sieve; wire together a small group of plants, then cover the wire with raffia. Finish off with a bow and glue the posy on to the sieve.

An old wooden bread board, some bread sticks and an array of dried flowers and grasses makes an original decoration for the kitchen. First drill a hole in the board about 3cm (1in) away from the edge. Thread a length of raffia through the hole and tie three bread sticks on to the board.

Next, make a posy out of small pink helichrysum (strawflower or everlasting), red berzilia and beard grass as follows. Wire together a tall group of plants using a long piece of silver wire. Add a second, slightly shorter, group to the bunch and bind it as before. Continue to add progressively shorter groups to the posy, binding at each stage with the same length of wire.

With the raffia, tie a second bundle of bread sticks to the board, at right angles to the first. Then tie the posy in position, finishing off with a raffia bow.

To preserve the singular colour of this serene arrangement, green marbles have been used in a green glass jug. Place the marbles in the jug — carefully — before adding the water. Then build up the basic outline with bear grass, allowing the blades to curve out on either side of the jug. Next, add about three bird of paradise leaves so that they curve out from the centre of the display.

Add two long stems of bells of Ireland and fill in the outline with *Leucodendron* foliage. To the front place a couple of pieces of variegated foliage — in this case *Euphorbia marginata*. This must be seared first to seal the stem (see page 8). In the small glass mug place water only and fill with a clump of *Euphorbia marginata*. This offsets the larger arrangement beautifully.

The warmth of natural wood is a perfect complement to the rich green tones of this display. First place a piece of cling film (plastic wrap) into the bowl to protect the wood from the water. Then tape a square brick of soaked florists' foam to a small saucer and place inside the salad bowl.

Arrange stems of foliage as shown, using small-leated eucalyptus and marguerite foliage. Let the stems curve up and out from the bowl, putting in plenty to act as a solid backdrop.

Sear some stems of variegated *Euphorbia marginata* (see page 8) and slot in among the other foliage somewhat randomly. Then 'sprinkle' about eight to 10 marguerites throughout the arrangement, lifting and highlighting the whole display.

Perfect for a special cocktail party! Cut the top from a large pineapple and slice a smaller pineapple in half lengthways. Scoop out the fruit and put soaked florists' foam into both pineapples. Insert fern fronds in the larger fruit to form the outline. Create the focal point with white lilies — shorter full flowers at the front, a longer stem at the back to give height.

A golden honeydew melon makes a practical and pretty container for flowers. Cut a wedge from the melon (just under a quarter) and scoop out most of the flesh from the fruit, putting it into the refrigerator to eat later! Insert a piece of soaked florists' foam into the fruit and slot in several stems of eucalyptus to create the outline.

Position a few daffodils first, cutting their stems on a slant to make them easier to insert into the foam. Keep all but one of the daffodils to roughly the same length, placing them on one side of the arrangement. Cut the last one shorter and put it in the foreground as the focal flower. On the opposite side to the daffodils insert two long stems of jonquil.

Bring more jonquil through the front of the display and recess a couple behind the focal daffodil. Add three purple hyacinth heads next, one either side of the focal daffodil, the other at the back to the left. Complete the picture with three white double tulips.

Complete the larger display with two stems of orange flowering *Euphorbia fulgens* and three orange tulips. Recess one tulip into the lilies. In the smaller pineapple place three additional orange tulips having cut them short so that they sit close to the foam. Add just one curving stem of flowering *Euphorbia* to the left of the display. Cocktail accessories add the finishing touch.

In this striking arrangement, a selection of natural coloured flowers and grasses has been chosen to complement the copper colours of the kettle. To begin, crush some wire mesh into a ball and place it inside the receptacle. Then build up the outline using plenty of black-eared barley.

Intersperse the arrangement with bleached white helichrysum (strawflower or everlasting) — these will add a welcome contrast to the browns and help to bring the display alive. Then add a few stems of moon grass.

To finish, add stems of clubrush throughout, recessing them deep into the arrangement to create depth. Try to keep the whole display light and airy with a slightly spiky effect.

A host of tiny dried flowers and grasses cluster round an old but gleaming brass bell, creating a very pretty effect. Cut a slice from a cylinder of florists' foam then cut the slice in half. Gouge out the centre of the two halves and affix the pieces to the handle as shown, using tape.

Build up the shape of the arrangement using single stems of mauve xeranthemum. Position those at the top of the display upright, and those lower down dangling over the bell. Now intersperse with wired clumps of quaking grass, following the same outline. Finish off with bunches of lady's mantle, pushed well into the arrangement.

Brass cow bells have been used to create this unusual display. Bind together several small bunches of dried flowers with silver wire. The pink bunch consists of gypsophila (baby's breath) and acroclinium (sunray); the yellow of oats, love-in-a-mist, and cluster-flowered helichrysum. Glue the bunches on to the bells, covering up the wires with short lengths of coloured cord.

Alternatively, you can glue the flowerheads directly on to the bell in a ring as shown here. These flowers are yellow helichrysum filled in with golden rod. Finally, tie a length of cord to one or more bells for hanging. Tie an extra little bunch of gypsophila half way up the cord for an added touch.

T his exquisite orange glass bowl is set off magnificiently with a selection of orchids. Place a piece of soaked florists' foam in the centre of the bowl and carefully surround it with marbles. This will hold the foam in position and prevent it from being seen through the glass. Begin with a group of long-stemmed *Arachnis* (scorpion) orchids, placing a couple at the back to establish the height.

Next, position a group of pale orange and white *Dendrobium* orchids in the front of the display reserving one or two to rise up at the back. Having filled the front of the bowl with *Dendrobium* orchids, create the focal point by adding three dark red *Cymbidium* orchids to the centre of the arrangement.

A stylish setting such as this modern yellow speckled fruit bowl really warrants creativity. Use contrasting colours and craft clever lines to achieve the best effects. Push half a brick of florists' foam well down into the bowl. Build up the outline with the tallest flowers — white stock and blue hyacinths — intermingling them.

To create the 'V' shape, arrange the red tulips and white 'rose' tulips alternatively in a diagonal line down one side of the display. Finish at the bottom with a red tulip, then work up the other side to complete the 'V'. Cover the visible foam with small pieces of lilac sea lavender and take longer sprays around the outline, trailing a little over the rim of the bowl.

This design combines flowers with candles to create a most attractive centrepiece for a dinner party. Use a wide-necked bowl, either glass or ceramic, and fill it with water to about 2cm (1in) below the rim. Then, snipping their stalks off close to the head, arrange some flowers on the surface of the water.

Flowers with large heads, such as the tulips and roses used here, are the easiest kind to float. But a few small orchids, with their interesting outline, add contrast to the arrangement.

This arrangement makes an ideal centrepiece for any table but especially a low coffee table where the pretty faces of the anemones can be seen to their best advantage. Half fill a clear glass bowl with water. Then select 12 to 15 anemones and cut their stems down to around 2-3cm (1-1½in).

Finally, add three or four floating candles. (Be careful not to overload the bowl with flowers, for they could catch fire once the candles are lit!)

Place the anemone heads on the surface of the water and intersperse with little clumps of *Viburnum tinus* to add contrast.

A second smaller bowl looks very attractive with the main arrangement and helps to break up the symmetry of the outline. Fill a smaller bowl with large shinning marbles and water. Then position just two or three anemone heads on the surface with a little sprig of gypsophila (also known as baby's breath in the United States) so that the marbles can still be seen.

T his sumptuous arrangement of plump flowers on a green glass cake stand looks almost edible! Place a round piece of soaked florists' foam in the centre of the stand. Then use yellow roses and alstroemeria alternately, cutting the stems on a slant and keeping them short so that once inserted into the foam the flower heads rest on the edge of the dish.

Finally, top the 'cake' with a few sprays of mimosa which will retain its pretty fluffy heads longer if conditioned first. This is done by submerging flower heads under cold water then dipping stems into 2.5cm (1in) of boiling water for a few seconds. Stand in a jug of warm water until the flowers have dried off.

The next layer comprises the bobbly 'flowers' of *Leucodendron brunia* followed by a ring of Persian buttercups. The latter will last longer if their stems are put into boiling water for a few seconds, before being given a long drink.

I n this continental-style arrangement, the different types of flowers are grouped together, rather than interspersed, to create a stunning effect on top of a simple glass cake stand. First, fix wet florists' foam to the cake stand using a plastic pin-holder.

Then, using long stems of *Liatris*, position several sprays upright at the back of the display and several more horizontally at the front, lying slightly to one side of the dish.

Group cream spray chrysanthemums to one side of the arrangement as shown, graduating their length so that the longest flower falls gently over the edge of the stand. Balance this with a stem or two on the opposite side of the arrangement to create continuity. Finally, fill in the centre and foreground with a group of lilac chrysanthemums.

Achieve a pleasing design with a green-tinged glass goblet and just three varieties of flowers. Carefully fill the goblet with marbles before adding the water. Start by positioning three bright crimson carnations to form the heart of the display. Then build up around them using five or six more carnations.

Fill in the outline with some alstroemeria and white lilac, hanging a stem of lilac gently over the rim of the glass. Complete the display with a few Portuguese laurel leaves. Remember that any display using marbles will shift slightly as you progress, so do not aim for too formal an arrangement — rather a more free-flowing one.

This natural yet graceful display consists of a mixture of spring flowers arranged in jam jars. A few coloured glass bottles have been added for contrast. A design such as this makes a very simple yet effective table centrepiece.

Here a squat clear jar is used for a mixture of white flowers and silvery-green foliage, forming a cool two-colour arrangement.

A single hyacinth is enough to fill the smaller jar, and the twisted stem of an anemone fits perfectly into a thin blue glass bottle. A colourful bunch of anemones in another jam jar completes the centrepiece.

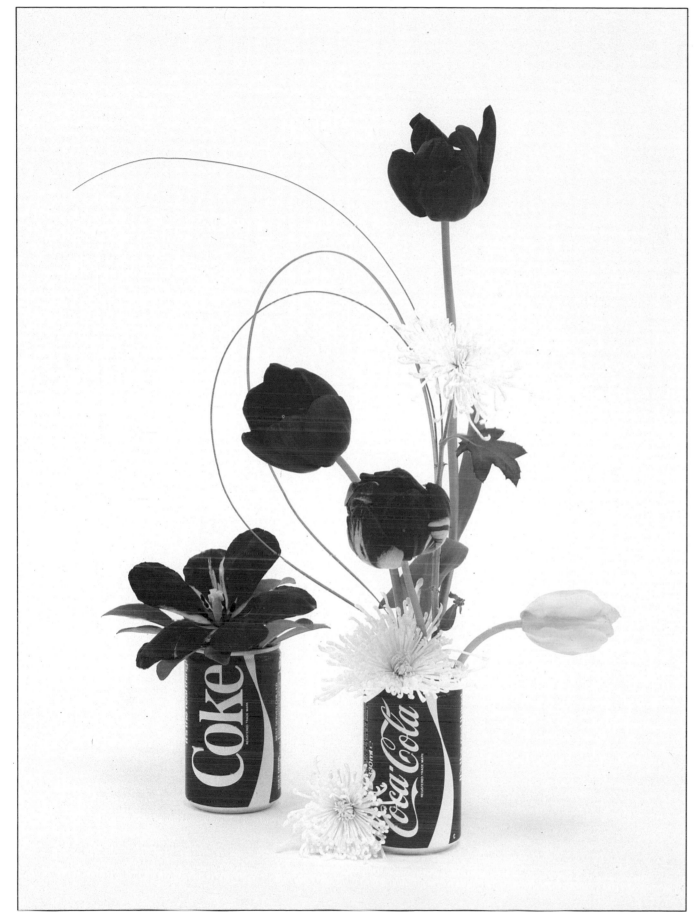

Put a couple of empty Coca-Cola cans to good use by creating this stunning linear arrangement. Take the tops off two cans with an opener and smooth down any rough edges. Put soaked florists' foam into both cans. To complement the design of the can use bold red and yellow tulips. Keep one red tulip tall, then graduate the height of the other tulips.

Position a cream spider chrysanthemum close to the can and one longer stem reaching halfway up the display. Then insert a little bear grass, looping the ends back into the can. Place one single red and yellow striped tulip — with its petals gently eased backwards — into the second can and finish off with a little foliage.

An attractive pink champagne bottle is offset with matching roses and delicate blossoms of broom. Half fill the bottle with water. A narrow-necked bottle is best with thin stems of flower sprays; so place just one stem of pink broom and one of small pink roses in the bottle. Cut the rose stem at an angle and trim off excess leaves so that only the stem is in the water.

As a perfect finish to the display add some delicate bear grass, bringing a couple of the blade ends back into the neck of the bottle to create the attractive loops. In the matching champagne glass carefully position a few marbles and fill with water. Place shorter sprays of broom and roses in the glass to complete the arrangement.

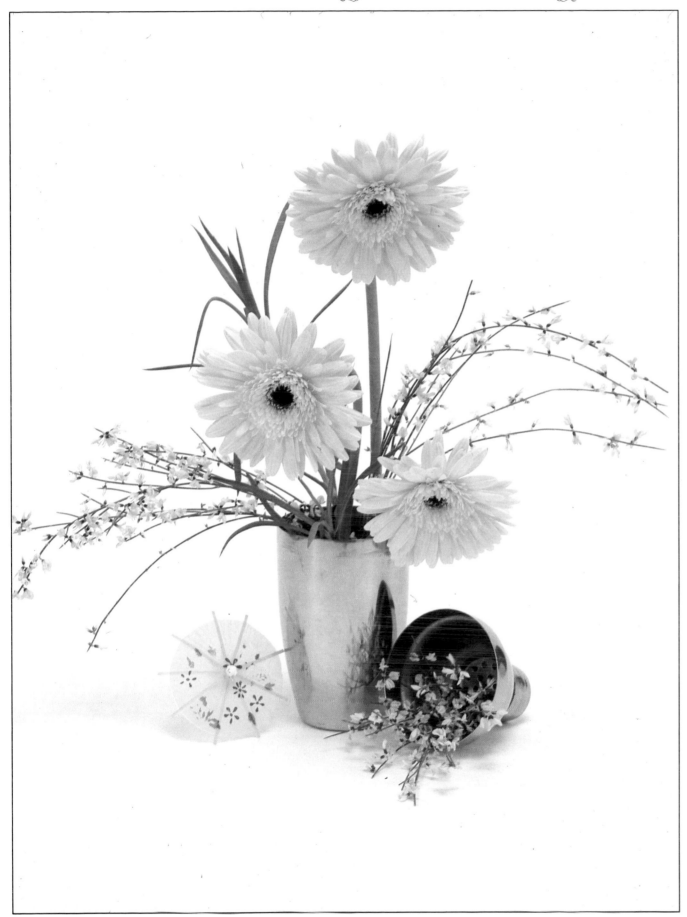

This highly effective arrangement only requires a cocktail shaker and flowers of one basic colour — a creamy yellow. Put a piece of soaked florists' foam into the shaker base, then insert three gerbera flowers, graduating the length of the stems. Add just a little foliage (in this case carnation foliage) behind and in front of the second tallest gerbera.

Position some curving sprays of yellow broom on either side of the display. The spiky flowers of the broom contrast with the soft petals of the gerbera. Reserve some short stems of broom and insert into a small piece of soaked florists' foam which has been positioned in the shaker lid. Place at the base of the main arrangement.

Old beer and medicine bottles make an attractive setting for a group of flowers or foliage. Because of their tight necks, only water (if fresh flowers are used) is necessary. Start by putting a spray and a single carnation flower into the central bottle.

Then add one or two stems of freesia to two of the other bottles. Create height by putting *Dendrobium* orchids and bird of paradise into a fourth bottle, allowing the latter to soar up above the other flowers. Complete the picture with a tiny orchid bloom in the smallest bottle.

A group of pretty little bottles in bright cobalt blue make an eye-catching setting for well-chosen flowers. Just put water into the bottles. Start with the tallest bottle at the back and fill with stems of delphinium and a little asparagus fern. In the bottle to the left, use shorter stems of miniature iris and yellow Persian buttercups.

In the central bottle place a small piece of *Euphorbia marginata* foliage, a stem of white stock and a single white freesia. This softens the bold primary colours picked up again by the blue-dyed yarrow in the bottle on the right. Complete the setting with two yellow Persian buttercups and a little mimosa in the smallest bottle at the front.

Picking up the Scottish theme of the pewter tankard, the deep rich reds and greens of this striking display cleverly echo a tartan design. Wedge left over scraps of soaked florists' foam into the tankard and then start the display with two bird of paradise leaves positioned at the rear.

A collection of pretty milk and cream jugs are enhanced by the addition of a few flowers. Place florists' foam into the larger jugs, just water into the smaller ones. Beginning with the central jug, fill it with stems of pink orchid and a little feathery asparagus fern.

Next, add several long stems of *Arachnis* (scorpion) orchids, fanning them out and above the bird of paradise leaves.

Insert taller stems of pink orchids into the jug at the back of the display and offset with white spray carnations. Take the carnations through the outline of both the back and central jugs so they create an effect of continuity.

Pick up the red in the stripes of the orchids with a dozen dark red spray chrysanthemums cut to varying heights. These form the focal point of the arrangement and help fill in the outline. This display is long-lasting providing the foam is watered regularly.

The mauve stripe in the jug on the left is picked up by three deep purple anemones. Add to this just a few sprigs of peach-coloured flowering *Euphorbia fulgens*. The *Euphorbia* is then continued in the tiny jug in the foreground. Balance the purple anemones with a bunch of blue-dyed yarrow in the last jug

Plain glass provides a most effective setting for the elegant contours of the arum lily (also known as calla lily). Fill the jar with small leafed eucalyptus, packing plenty in to hold the wide heavy stems of the arum lilies. Place a few sprays of eucalyptus at the back to establish the height and insert several arum lilies of graduating heights among the foliage, following the outline.

Fill in the outline with four shaggy-edged peach carnations and four tiny white roses. Although the carnations appear as the focal point of the display, they also serve as a sharp contrast to the arum lilies and help set both flowers off to their best advantage. A little eucalyptus and a peach carnation in the smaller jar balances the larger display.

This oblong glass vase displays all the individual varieties of flowers prominently. Fill the vase with marbles then with water. Position the purple iris first, taking stems of similar length and placing them so that they lean on one side of the vase.

Because the marbles shift slightly as you insert the stems, it is usually easier to work from one side of the vase to the other. So next take the grey *Kochia* (summer cypress) foliage and place alongside the irises to the back of the vase. In front of the *Kochia* group some pink nerines.

Position several mid-blue scabious (known as pincushion flowers in the United States) of varying length next, and finally, four or five bright pink hyacinths to complete the arrangement.

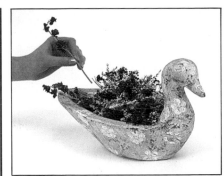

This 'marble-effect' duck is actually made from papier maché and would, therefore, be ruined by the use of water. Consequently, an attractive display of dried plants has been arranged inside it. Place some dry florists' foam into the duck and cover with purple and white flowers such as sea lavender and larkspur.

Fill in the 'plumage' with more lilac-coloured sea lavender. This plant is easily obtainable from most florists and is a useful and pretty base for many dried arrangements. It comes in numerous 'new art shades' of salmon, orange, yellow, carmine, blue and lavender.

A novel toothbrush holder and soap dish are ideal for bathroom flower displays. Beginning with the toothbrush holder, fill it with water and place a small group of *Brodiaea* to one side. Follow with a group of pink nerines in the centre, and then add more *Brodiaea*. Back the display with a little naturally dried sea lavender.

For the soap-bearing duck use a pin-holder to secure some florists' foam to the dish. Then fill the dish with the tops of hyacinths, cutting the stems at an angle with a sharp knife as they are quite thick and otherwise unmanageable. (This is a good way of using up hyacinths once the bottom parts have started to die.)

Complete the duck's plumage with other dried grasses such as the plump, fluffy *Lagurus* (also known as rabbit or hare's tail grass) and the feathery *Agrostis pulchella* which creates a 'tail'. Lilac ribbons inserted among the arrangement enhance the display.

Complete the arrangement in the soap holder with a few *Brodiaea* florets and sprigs of sea lavender.

Make the most of unusual vegetables. Here, the centre of a squash is scooped out to create two unusual containers. Put some soaked florists' foam into both 'skins'. Form a 'pyramid' with *Choisya ternata* foliage in the main piece of squash and add a few fern fronds. From this mass of foliage extend ten to twelve tulips in contrasting colours of orange and red and yellow stripes.

Into the display recess several cream spider chrysanthemums. These come in sprays but the individual flowers on their own short 'stems' are perfect for creating depth.

Fill in the outline with seven or eight white iris. For the top of the squash use stems of 'Huckleberry' and *Choisya* foliage to form an outline and fill in with a simple mixture of cream spider and rust-coloured daisy chrysanthemums. These colours beautifully complement the main arrangement.

A dustpan is, perhaps, not generally considered as a container for flowers but, as this design shows, such a utensil can make an attractive setting for a low-lying arrangement of bright spring flowers. Tape some soaked florists' foam to a saucer and place in the dustpan. Cover the foam with *Choisya ternata* foliage.

Begin to create the outline with fern fronds, extending them beyond the *Choisya* foliage. Then use bright yellow daffodils of similar length to form a strong diagonal line across the display, lying parallel to the shorter line already established by the fern fronds.

Strengthen this outline with orange tulips, extending them beyond the daffodils in all directions, yet keeping the general strong diagonal line intact. Gently open one tulip in the centre to create a focal point. Fill in the outline with stems of peach coloured flowering *Euphorbia fulgens*, recessing a few stems to give depth.

Brighten up an obsolete typewriter by using it as a background for some cheerful spring flowers. Begin by taping some soaked florists' foam onto a small saucer and placing into the 'well' of the typewriter keys. Cut the stems of a few full-blooming white lilies in graduating heights and insert into the foam. Position a lily bud to rise at the back of the display.

Next, take six yellow tulips and fill in the outline formed by the lilies. For co-ordinating colour, yet contrasting texture, recess several stems of fluffy mimosa. Note how effectively the cream and gold of the flowers are reflected in the typewriter keys.

This battered old watering can has been given a new lease of life as part of an imaginative arrangement of dried flowers, cereals and grasses. Begin by packing wire mesh into the neck of the can.

Start to build up the shape of the display with tall bundles of black-eared barley, putting them both sides of the handle. It is not necessary to wire the barley. Next scatter purple xeranthemums throughout, keeping some stems quite short, others as tall as the barley.

Continue to fill out the display using plenty of yellow-dyed *Lagurus* (rabbit's or hare's tail grass). Add the grass singly and concentrate it around the base of the arrangement so that it helps to cover the top of the watering can. Add depth to the display with long stems of brown 'blue leaf', following the general outline.

When you are happy with the shape of the arrangement, put a few xeranthemums and ears of barley into the spout so that they look as if they are spilling out. To finish, plait three lengths of raffia. Using an extra strand of raffia, fix the plait into a bow shape and tie it on to the handle of the watering can.

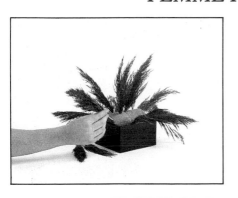

This dark and moody dried arrangement makes an interesting change from the more usual brightly coloured displays. It is set within a shiny black plastic box designed for office use. Begin by packing two circular pieces of florists' foam into the box — this will give height to the centre of the arrangement. Next build up the shape with reed.

A wooden biscuit barrel sets off an unusually dark arrangement of dried plants to perfection. First pack the barrel with a length of wire mesh.

Add a hint of red with long stems of rat's tail statice scattered in amongst the reed. Try to keep the height of the two plants about the same.

Build up a fan-shaped outline using stems of *Leucodendron*, then fill in the remaining gaps with clumps of red berzilia. The stems of both plants are fairly strong so there should be no need to wire them.

Wire together clumps of South African daisies (a type of helichrysum) and insert them deep into the arrangement. These add welcome highlights to the display and bring it to life.

Finally, add some stems of apricot glabrum cones, positioning them mainly in the centre of the arrangement to act as the focal point. Keep the stems short so that they sit deep in amongst the other plants, giving substance to the display.

A handsome old stoneware filter jar is a handy container for flowers, but a whole brick of florists' foam is needed for the arrangement because of the jar's height. Begin with sprays of sprengeri fern, trailing some stems over the sides of the jar. In the centre and to the back add long stems of white lilac. To strengthen the outline add some white stock.

Pink stock, pink roses and pink tulips dominate the display. Just a little pink stock is needed as the main flowers are the roses and the tulips. Position these throughout the display, keeping a fairly symmetrical design. The lid of the jar propped up at the base creates the finishing touch.

This charming informal arrangement is proof that flowers can be arranged effectively in all sorts of containers. The two containers shown here are a pretty floral mug and a wide cup and saucer, the kind used for breakfast coffee in France.

Tulips are usually arranged in a tall vase, but here they are treated more informally, grouped in a pretty mug. Cut the stems short to suit the container, but don't discard the leaves — arrange them in among the flowers. The breakfast cup is first partially filled with freesias.

A few carefully placed anemones add colour to the arrangement and also help to link it with the tulips in the other container.

An old fashioned set of scales provides an eye-catching setting for flowers and foliage. Position a piece of soaked florists' foam into the pan of the scales and insert several stems of *Leucodendron.* Follow the outline of the scales' weighing pan with the foliage, ensuring that the foam is virtually covered.

Create the focal point using alstroemeria. Keep the stems slightly longer than the *Leucodendron,* slotting them in between the foliage so that their 'faces' look up and out from the pan.

Recess two types of dried yarrow into the arrangement to provide depth and a contrast of texture. The yellow also complements the golden streaks in the alstroemeria. To finish, add a little spray of yarrow and an alstroemeria flower sitting alongside the weights to create continuity for the eye.

Old polished wood is a perfect backdrop for any flowers, enhancing their shape and colour. Wrap cling film (plastic wrap) around some florists' foam and place in the lower drawer. Pack the drawer with forget-me-nots and a little *Brodiaea.* To the left place a little clump of *Viburnum tinus* and a tiny spider chrysanthemum. Place a few pink miniature roses to the right.

Fill the second drawer with roses and their buds, once again using florists' foam based with cling film (plastic wrap). The main mass of pink roses should appear from the left hand side of the drawer. This forms an optical line with the roses in the bottom drawer. Complete with sprigs of forget-me-nots and *Viburnum tinus* peeping out of the top drawer.

Transform a copper colander with an unusual display of dried plants. In this arrangement, gold and russets have been chosen to reflect the colour of both bowl and fruit. Begin by rolling a length of wire mesh into a tube about 3cm (1in) in diameter and fixing it into one half of the bowl. Now place wired bunches of dudinea into the mesh to build up the shape.

Wire together a few groups of Chinese lantern — about four to five heads per group — and place these in amongst the dudinea.

Add about two to three wired bunches of millet, allowing them to droop across the arrangement and over the sides of the bowl. You don't need to use many stems to get the desired effect. Finally, put the fruit into the bowl, adding a last piece of dudinea at the front to complete the picture.

A jet black wooden box provides a frame for this pretty dried arrangement, and helps to bring out the subtle warmth of the roses. Cut a block of florists' foam to fit the box and wedge it tightly in place. If the fit is good there should be no need to tape it.

Build up the outline using wired bunches of white bupleurum. Keep the shape well within that of the box. Start to fill in the outline with South African daisies (a type of helichrysum), using them to cover the foam. Make the flowers shorter at the front of the display, slightly overhanging the edge of the box.

Complete the picture with several rust-coloured roses, recessing some deep into the arrangement. Gently pull back the outer petals if necessary to open out the flowers before you position them.

A few gnarled twigs give this attractive dried arrangement an oriental quality. Begin by making a moss base. Mould some wire mesh into a tube, fill it with dry moss and close the ends. Pack this into a small wicker basket, securing it with wire. Now insert a few twisted willow twigs, mainly at the sides, to form an unusual shape. Add some white proteus next, and a few grasses.

Use the grass to form the main outline, keeping the stems quite tall at the back. Now begin to fill in with small yellow helichrysum (strawflower or everlasting) and add highlights to the display with a few wired clumps of bleached white helichrysum. For contrasting textures, add a few cones and finish off with stems of canella,

Employ the picnic hamper, before the summer comes, as a setting for groups of spring flowers. Place some soaked florists' foam on a dinner plate and fit into the hamper. Prop open the lid at a fairly wide angle with a small stick. 'Line' the basket with Portuguese laurel and begin grouping the flowers. Start with just two white lilies in the bottom right hand corner.

Next, arrange several orange tulips, in a diagonal line extending from the tip of the basket lid to the left edge of the basket handle.

Add clumps of white lilac to fill the centre of the display, removing nearly all the foliage first. (To condition the lilac, hammer the stem ends really well before giving them a long drink in warm water.)

Next, group a bunch of three or four purple iris beside the lilac, and finally add another cluster of tulips, this time yellow ones to complement the rest of the design. Complete the display with fern fronds and variegated ivy trailing from the front of the basket.

There is nothing quite like a mass of flowers and, here, armfuls of pink tulips set against a black plastic basket look simply stunning. Put a heavy container into the shopping basket to weight it down, then fill the container with water. Add numerous tulips of varying shades of pink — the more flowers the better. Position them sweeping out of the basket in a fairly random fashion.

Little else is needed in this type of wanton arrangement. Just add a touch of laurel foliage as a contrast to all the tulips. Before displaying the laurel, hammer the stems first, then give them a long drink of water.

Adelightful idea for Easter, these pretty floral baskets are easy to make and will last much longer than cut flowers. First line the basket with a piece of plastic, using black for a dark twig basket or white for a light-coloured willow basket.

Add a layer of damp sphagnum moss. This will provide a base for your pots of flowers, lifting them to the correct height for the basket. It also prevents the roots of the plants from drying out. (Check the moss occasionally to make sure it is still damp; if not, sprinkle it with water to dampen it.)

Now arrange the pots on top of the layer of moss, adjusting them as necessary so that they sit straight and create a symmetrical arrangement. Alternate yellow and white primroses for the best effect.

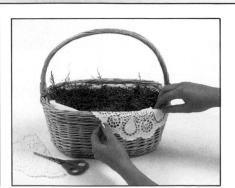

You can leave the basket plain or, as shown here, add a paper doily for a pretty trim. Cut two doilies in half and fold the edge of each half around the rim of the basket before inserting the pots.

Here, a wicker waste-paper basket forms the basis of an attractive arrangement of ferns and carnations. Note how the colour of the basket has been picked out in the flowers to create a stunning effect. Begin by taping soaked florists' foam into a container and positioning it inside the basket. Then fan out the fern fronds to form the setting for the flowers.

Take white spray carnations and intersperse them among the shorter fern fronds at the front, placing a few longer stems towards the back. Do the same with the bright red carnations.

Tie ribbons around the handle of the basket to provide the finishing touch. A smaller basket filled with freesias and narcissi add a charming contrast to the arrangement. Line the basket with black plastic as before, then insert a chunk of soaked florists' foam into which the flowers can be inserted.

Finish off by adding a sprinkling of September flowers (a form of aster) to soften the whole effect. (This display can also be achieved by pushing tiny phials of flowers into the soil of a real fern, such an arrangement being known as a pot-et-fleurs — see page 15).

To create this vibrant dried arrangement, first make a moss base for the basket. Roll some wire mesh into a tube, pack it with dry moss and close the ends. Squash the base into the basket and wire it in place as shown. Begin to form the outline of the arrangement with bleached white helichrysum (strawflower or everlasting), creating a dome shape.

Continue to build up the shape with white proteus. Add some clubrush next, followed by a number of cones, such as these meridianum. The colour of these two plants cleverly picks up the brown in the basket. Complete the display with bright yellow clumps of cressia and cluster-flowered helichrysum. Place them low down in the arrangement, filling in the gaps between the other plants.

A small wicker basket holds a cheerful display of tiny dried flowers. Begin by packing the base of the basket with wire mesh, wiring it to the rim to hold it in position. Fix the lid open using a piece of thick wire as a prop. Now form a base for the display using sea lavender, arranging it loosely throughout the mesh.

Fill in the display with wired clumps of yellow silver-leaved helichrysum, keeping it tight and slightly lower than the sea lavender. Add a splash of colour with small clumps of red helichrysum, breaking out of the shape a little with some taller pieces at the back.

Add groups of small red roses, concentrating them in groups, some bursting out of the sides of the arrangement, others spilling over the front. A few poppy heads add contrast of texture — insert about three bunches, keeping them tall so that they stand out above the other flowers. Finish off with stems of brown 'blue leaf', fanning them out on one side as shown above.

A dark, rustic basket cradles a wild and colourful display of dried plants. Begin by placing a large block of florists' foam inside the basket. Run a couple of wires across the top to hold the foam in place, securing the ends of the wires to the rim of the basket.

Build up the outline of the display with wired clumps of love-in-a-mist, allowing some of the flowerheads to droop over the sides of the basket. Next, slot in single stems of bottlebrush at varying heights to give rich red tones to the display.

Add bright yellow highlights by inserting wired clumps of yarrow throughout. Finally, arrange some long stems of blue larkspur, keeping them slightly taller than the other plants.

The warmth of polished wood provides a beautiful backdrop for a floral display. Here the lustrous sheen of Portuguese laurel highlights the natural shine of an old wooden artist's box. Tape soaked florists' foam to a plate before inserting into the box — this will protect the wood from any water spillage.

Prop open the box with a small stick or twig. Now create the outline with Portuguese laurel, covering the foam and filling the open box.

Bright yellow double tulips are positioned next. Cut them all to approximately the same length, on the slant so that they slot into the foam more easily. Place them throughout the display. To create depth, recess several cream spider chrysanthemums, their 'feathery' heads providing a contrast of shape and texture to the rather solid lines of the other flowers.

To complete the arrangement add the focal flowers — the white lilies. Their orangey-brown pollen enhances the wood while the yellow specks on the inside of their petals highlights the boldly-coloured tulips.

To highlight the pattern on these pretty containers, the gold of the decanter has been cleverly picked out by the choice of flowers in the display. Begin by spraying dried love in a mist seed heads with gold paint. When dry, insert a number of sprays into the vessel, varying their height to create an outline. Reserve a few for the small jug.

Add three white full carnations to form the focal point of the arrangement and complement the gold. Help fill in the outline with orchid sprays, pointing them downward towards the smaller jug which can then be filled with a few dried and sprayed love in a mist.

This simple but effective arrangement of flowers and foliage is held in place by the tight neck of the decanter which, in turn, restricts the number of plants in the display. Begin by filling the vessel with water and positioning three wild garlic flowerheads at graduating heights.

Then add a few fern fronds as shown here, and trail a stem of variegated ivy down in front of the decanter. Finally, position the focal flowers — three cream spray chrysanthemums — putting two short ones close to the rim of the decanter with one taller one behind. The cream is the dominant colour of the arrangement, picked up in the chrysanthemums, the garlic and the ivy.

Verging on the ridiculous, this amusing idea is nonetheless highly effective. Place some soaked florists' foam into two small wine glasses and slot one into each boot. Begin by placing some feathery sprengai fern into the blue boot. Strengthen this outline with a few daffodils and stems of jonquil.

Add a beautiful white iris to form the focal point of the display in the blue boot. Then position two taller iris at the back, along with two white lily buds. For contrasting texture, and to create depth and substance, add a few curving stems of white lilac.

In the red boot create the outline with blue iris and a single blue hyacinth. Then add red and yellow/red striped tulips, allowing them to break out of the outline and curve gently away to follow the foot of the boot. Recess some stems of white lilac into the display and complete with four or five bright red spray carnations, keeping them close to the heart of the arrangement.

A child's toy is possibly one of the least likely containers for flowers but this yellow truck provides a novel way of setting off bright orange blooms. Place a saucer of soaked florists' foam into the truck. Cover the foam with *Choisya ternata* foliage and add some orange spray chrysanthemums, picking up the colour of the bright stripes in the toy.

Fill in the outline with orange spray carnations. Next insert the focal flowers — four or five orange tulips. Keep their stems quite long so that they stand above the dense mass of foliage and other flowers. (Tulips last longer if first conditioned in a vase of water into which has been added a teaspoonful of sugar.)

Recess some cream spider chrysanthemums into the arrangement to create depth and for contrasting texture. Finally, offset the display with bright yellow Persian buttercups liberally spread throughout the display.

Old, well-preserved toys which still hold sentimental value can be put to good use as flower holders. The flowers even hide the dents and scratches! This wooden toy train with its little carriages makes an appealing display. Begin by wrapping some soaked florists' foam in cling film (plastic wrap) and placing it into the train's carriages.

Fill the first carriage with short stems of 'Huckleberry' foliage and insert five or six closely cut daisy chrysanthemums.

Add a few orange carnations flecked with red and recess some peach-coloured flowering *Euphorbia fulgens,* remembering to sear it first (see page 8). The tiny flowers and rich foliage of the *Euphorbia* give substance and depth to the 'posy'.

In the second carriage, begin the display with a single orange tulip, gently easing back its petals to give a more open effect. Surround the tulip with more 'Huckleberry' foliage and finish off with peach-coloured flowering *Euphorbia.*

An old candy jar has been used for the basis of this beautiful display, and the marbles, though used predominantly to hold the arrangement in position, add a pretty touch to the overall effect. Build up the outline with the mimosa, then add several stems of purple iris at varying heights as shown.

Use yellow roses to form the focal point, positioning one or two slightly off centre for balance. Add a few sprays of lemon-cream statice — longer stems at the side, shorter ones close to the rim of the jar — to provide a contrast of texture and complement the rich yellow of the mimosa and roses.

Finally, put three or four white carnations among the arrangement, recessing one or two smaller ones. These help to break up the solid mass of yellow. A little spray of mimosa, positioned on the glass stopper at the foot of the jar, adds the finishing touch.

Pretty floral displays in two small but sturdy house plant containers serve as excellent book ends. Put well-soaked florists' foam into the pots. Then check that the pots are heavy enough to support the books. It would be a great pity to complete the arrangements only to find that the books knock over all your hard work and creativity!

Arrange the flowers in such a way that each display has a 'flat' side which can be put up against the books. Taking the first pot begin by filling it with sprengeri fern, creating a diagonal outline.

Follow the outline with rust-coloured spray chrysanthemums, then add the focal point using white double tulips. Use three or four tulips of differing heights, taking them through the centre of the display.

Fill in the outline with yellow Persian buttercup buds and flowers. (These will last longer if properly conditioned first: put the ends of the stems into boiling water for a few seconds before giving them a long drink.) To complete the picture, similarly arrange the flowers in the second pot, creating a 'flat' surface on the opposite side to that in the first display.

EASTER BONNET

TOP HAT

Here is a novel way of utilizing a pretty straw hat which is too small or past its prime. Tape some soaked florists' foam to a saucer and place in the hat. Create a soft and spidery outline with stems of sprengeri fern. Next, take three or four stems of white stock and insert into the heart of the display, bringing just one stem forward over the brim of the hat.

Use white daisy chrysanthemums to fill in the outline and give substance to the design. (These flowers are generally good survivors when cut, but they will last even longer if the stem ends are placed into boiling water first before being left in deep water for a long drink.)

In among the chrysanthemums recess some lilac hyacinth heads to create depth and a contrasting texture. Finally, complete the display with deep purple anemones. These are the main flowers, so use plenty, spreading them evenly throughout the arrangement.

A party or special event is a good excuse for an unusual 'thematic' display. This one might go well at a theatrical gathering — or even a wedding! Begin by putting a large brick of soaked florists' foam into a container which will fit comfortably into the hat. Fan out sprays of *Mallalika* foliage and fill in with September flowers (a form of aster).

Recess white spray chrysanthemums into the foliage and use longer stems to establish the height towards the back. Have a couple trailing over the brim of the hat alongside a few of the September flowers.

The focal point of the arrangement is poinsettia flowers which should be conditioned first by searing the stem ends with a lighted candle (see page 8). Fill in the outline and balance the display with deep red spray carnations.

Keep the champagne in the refrigerator and use the ice bucket for red roses! First, put soaked florists' foam at the base of the bucket. Then insert some variegated foliage — shown here is a spine-less form of holly. Intersperse this with eight or nine red roses, still in bud. Have two or three longer stems rising from the foliage to one side at the back.

Fill in all the available space with jonquil, following the outline. The gold is highlighted by the yellow-edged foliage. (A handy tip: the roses will last longer if the stems are placed in boiling water for a minute before being given a long drink.)

The swirling design on a pretty chamber pot is picked up by the arrangement within it, an effect which can be achieved with any attractively patterned container. Begin with the yellows — Ti tree, lady's mantle, golden rod and yarrow — keeping the arrangement informal and natural. Next, add some light brown dried sea lavender and safflower.

The red-headed safflower will pick up the colours from the pot's design. Then add some dried brown grasses and brown seed heads, keeping the arrangement wide and full.

What better way of displaying a pretty dried arrangement and keeping it dust-free than under a glass cheese dome? Fix dry florists' foam to the base with a plastic pin-holder. Cover the foam with dried hydrangea heads, some of which have been previously part-sprayed with gold paint. Add some brown-dyed protea twigs and seed-heads.

The most fragile plants — honesty and Chinese lanterns — should be added last. These give the arrangement body and contrasting texture as well as off-setting the glorious orangey-reds in the pattern of the pot.

To make the arrangement asymmetrical, add the orange-dyed statice on one side to form a gentle curve which sweeps down and away from the focal point — the helichrysum (strawflower or everlasting). Keep the pretty 'faces' of the helichrysum looking up and out, with the more orange-coloured ones close to the orange statice.

Complete the arrangement with two varieties of yarrow, slotting them among the hydrangea opposite the statice. The mustard-coloured yarrow not only enhances the autumnal effect of the arrangement but adds a soft texture. (Yarrow is an easy plant to preserve as it dries quickly without water.)

The rough hessian of coffee sacks provides a good background material for this dried display. Put dry florists' foam into the first sack and fill out with crushed newspaper or tissue. Cover the foam with yellow and brown-dyed sea leavender, then add grains and grasses such as wild oats, *Phalaris* and wheat. Bells of Ireland also add interest, texture and height.

Build up the design with brown plants such as Ti-tree, *Stirlingia, Leptocarpus,* dried protea and *Gynerium.*

Tiny cones on twigs and preserved eucalyptus add interesting textures and colours to the display, and there are many more grasses and dried materials that can be added to complete the picture.

Another sack, similarly packed with foam and crushed paper, achieves a different effect with the addition of teasels, brown-dyed sea lavender and sunray.

Most flower arrangements look well against a natural setting. Here, coral is used as a base for freesias and *Oncidium ornithorhynchum* orchids. Wrap a piece of soaked florists' foam in cling film (plastic wrap) and place it behind the coral. Then pass the freesia stems through the coral branches and insert into the foam.

Finally, pass longer stems of *Oncidium* orchids through the back and sides of the coral and into the foam. Only one or two flower varieties will be needed with a complex container such as coral.

Not exactly a horn of plenty, but a conch shell with flowers, foliage and coral spilling out to form an attractive and exotic 'marine' display. To begin, wrap some soaked florists' foam in cling film (plastic wrap) and push it into the hole of the shell. (Cling film is used to prevent fragments of foam getting lost inside the shell).

Next, add some 'flowing' foliage — this *Leucodendron* resembles seaweed and is perfect for this arrangement. The peach spray carnations match the colour on the shell. Have these peeping out, following the flowing outline created by the foliage.

For dramatic contrast intersperse some brick red carnations among the peach ones, recessing one or two. Add a contrast of texture in the form of two pieces of flat coral. To complete the arrangement, arrange two long stems of striped *Arachnis* (scorpion) orchid flowing out from the shell and strengthening the outline.

SEASCAPE

IKEBANA

A goldfish bowl is one item that many people have tucked away, judging by the average lifespan of most goldfish! Put the bowl to good use by creating a really eye-catching arrangement. Fill the bowl carefully with a mixture of shells and pebbles before adding the water.

The aim is to achieve a 'waterspray' effect with the first few flowers. Start with gypsophila (also known as baby's breath in the United States), trailing a little over the side. Next add stems of delicate blue *Brodiaea*, following the same outline.

Peach spray carnations reflect the colour in some of the shells and only a few are needed to follow the sweeping outline already established. Dried onion heads have a lovely texture and their colour is picked up by the pebbles and shells. Place eight or so throughout the arrangement, filling in the outline.

D rift or bog wood — with its natural contours — provides an ideal setting for this unusual display. Take three pieces of flat coral and insert them into a lump of soaked florists' foam which has been wrapped in cling film (plastic wrap) and attached to the wood with wire.

Position a single gerbera bloom to sit in the centre of the display, obscuring the foam and creating a focal point. Add two stems of *Arachnis* (scorpion) orchid — one at the back, the other shorter piece lying forwards — to complete the picture.

Alarge piece of bark forms part of a colourful display of oranges, creams and browns. Choose a piece of bark with a good shape and interesting, gnarled features. Start by moulding some wire mesh into a tube and filling it with moss. Attach this to the bark using lengths of wire. Bore small holes in the sides of the bark to secure the wire if necessary.

Begin to build up the shape of the arrangement using wired clumps of dudinea. Scatter them throughout the moss base, keeping the shape low and well within the outline of the bark. Next add clumps of bright yellow cluster-flowered helichrysum (strawflower or everlasting), followed by groups of bobbly *Leucodendron brunia*.

Wire together bunches of large helichrysum, choosing a range of colours, and use these to fill in the arrangement, still keeping the shape low and compact. For contrast, add stems of brown 'blue leaf', allowing some to break out of the outline.

To soften the effect, arrange clumps of golden rod throughout. Then finish off with a few wired stems of oats.

This aromatic pomander contains a range of interesting spices and makes an unusual kitchen decoration. Begin by plaiting three strands of raffia. Join the ends with a long piece of wire, then push the wire through a sphere of florists' foam, doubling it back on itself to secure. Wire bunches of cinnamon and Spanish root (liquorice stick) and conceal the wires with thin strands of raffia.

The other two spices used are star-shaped aniseed and white lomius. Wire these also and cover the foam with the spices, trying to keep the shape roughly spherical. Now insert clumps of small poppy heads, filling in the gaps between the spices.

A small block of cork bark forms the base for an attractive display of neutral-coloured dried plants. Begin by cutting a piece of florists' foam down to a size that will sit comfortably on the middle of the bark. Tape the foam in place.

Build up the outline of the display with single stems of green amaranthus (love-lies-bleeding). Create a spiky effect, with some of the plants trailing over the edges of the bark. Fill in with *Leucodendron*, keeping the stems shorter than those of the amaranthus so that the plants lie lower down in the arrangement.

Add some large poppy heads for contrast. Insert them singly but arrange them in groups of two or three, standing out from the other plants. Finally, add a few dark cones to add depth to the arrangement those used here are platyspernum cones.

To finish, add a few highlights with several small wired bunches of ammobium (sandflower or winged everlasting), concentrating them in the centre of the display.

Zany gift bags in shiny metallic colours provide an eye-catching setting. Take three bags of varying size and colour. Put one small sherry or wine glass into each of the smaller bags and two glasses in the larger bag. Put some soaked florists' foam into the glasses. Start with the pink bag and arrange graduatings stems of blue flowers: *Dendrobium* orchids, blue-dyed yarrow and grape hyacinths.

To complete the pink bag add one blue-dyed carnation. Three pale pink double tulips beautifully offset the blue of both the bag and flowers. Cut them to differing heights and position in the blue bag. Continue the blue by placing three dyed carnations in the silver bag. Crushed tissue paper, some satin ribbon and a single pink nerine completes the pictures.

Frothy strawberry and vanilla ice cream colours spill from this little attaché case. Begin by wrapping a brick of soaked florists' foam in cling film (plastic wrap) and fit it into the case. Form the outline with small-leafed eucalyptus; into this recess four or five white spray chrysanthemums. Position some stems of white stock to one side of the case to establish the height.

Next, gather two shades of pink net into small bunches and secure at the base with wire. Place two or three net bunches at the back of the display and one small piece at the front in the corner. Then, following the outline, put pale pink spray carnations throughout the arrangement.

For the focal point use single deep pink carnations. Trail two sprays of *Dendrobium* orchids from the two front corners of the case. Finally, fill out the outline with pink-dyed sea lavender.

Sunny yellow provides a perfect backdrop for these bright spring yellows and lilacs. Prop open the lid of the case with a small stick and insert a brick of soaked florists' foam wrapped in cling film (plastic wrap). Begin by grouping some closely cut white iris to the right of the case, standing them upright at the back. Next to them insert a bunch of white net.

In front of the iris, group eight to ten yellow Persian buttercups and a touch of foliage. Six or seven white double tulips fill virtually the rest of the case. On the far left of the case, and in among the tulips, slot three or four purple hyacinths. For the finishing touch add a little piece of lilac net, bunched on some wire, in the top right hand corner to balance the colour scheme.

The following is an alphabetical list of the common names of plants
used in this section and their Latin equivalents.

Common name	Latin name	Common name	Latin name	Common name	Latin name	Common name	Latin name
Acroclinium (sunray)	*Acroclinium roseum = Helipterum roseum*	Dumb cane	*Dieffenbachia*	Lily	*Lilium*	Rhodanthe (a type of sunray, also called Swan River everlasting)	*Rhodanthe manglesii = Helipterum manglesii*
		Eucalyptus	*Eucalyptus*	Love-in-a-mist	*Nigella damascena*		
Alstroemeria	*Alstroemeria*	Fern (Boston)	*Nephrolepis exaltata*	Love-lies-bleeding	*Amaranthus caudatus*		
(also called Peruvian lily)		Forget-me-not	*Myosotis sylvatica*	Marguerite	*Chrysanthemum*	Rose	*Rosa*
Amaryllis	*Hippeastrum aulicum*	Forsythia	*Forsythia*	Mimosa	*Acacia*	Safflower	*Carthamus tinctorius*
Anemone	*Anemone*	Freesia	*Freesia*	Mock orange blossom	*Philadelphus*	Sandflower	*Ammobium alatum*
Arum lily	*Zantedeschia aethiopica*	Garlic	*Allium sativum*	Nerine	*Nerine*	(also called winged everlasting)	
(also called calla lily)		Gerbera	*Gerbera*	Nipplewort	*Laspana communis*		
Asparagus fern	*Asparagus plumosis*	Gladiolus	*Gladiolus*	(also called broom bloom)		Scabious	*Scabiosa*
Barley, black-eared	*Hordeum*	Golden rod	*Solidago*	Oats, wild	*Avena fatua*	(also called pincushion flower)	
Beard grass	*Polypogon*	Grape hyacinth	*Muscari*	Onion	*Allium cepa*	Sea lavender	*Limonium tataricum = Goniolimon tataricum*
Beech	*Fagus sylvatica*	Gypsophila	*Gypsophila*	Oregon grape	*Mahonia aquifolium*		
Bells of Ireland	*Moluccella laevis*	(also called baby's breath)		Pearl everlasting	*Anaphalis*	September flower	*Aster ericoides*
Bird of Paradise	*Strelitzia reginae*	Heather	*Erica*	Peony	*Paeonia lactiflora*	Snapdragon	*Antirrhinum*
Bottlebrush	*Callistemon*	Holly	*Ilex aquifolium*	Persian buttercup	*Ranunculus asiaticus*	Spindle tree	*Euonymus europaeus*
Bouvardia	*Bouvardia*	Honesty	*Lumnaria annua*	Poinsettia	*Euphorbia pulcherrima*	Spotted laurel	*Aucuba japonica*
Broom	*Genista*	(also called silver dollar plant)		Poppy	*Papaver*	Sprengeri fern	*Asparagus sprengeri*
Capsicum	*Capsicum*	Huckleberry	*Gaylussacia*	Portuguese laurel	*Prunus lusitanica*	Statice	*Limonium sinuatum*
(also called Christmas pepper)		Hyacinth	*Hyacinthus*	Primrose	*Primula variablis*	Strawflower or everlasting	*Helichrysum*
Carnation	*Dianthus*	Hydrangea	*Hydrangea*	Quaking grass	*Briza maxima*	Summer cypress	*Kochia scoparia*
Chinese lantern	*Physalis alkekengi*	Iris	*Iris*	Rabbit's or hare's tail grass	*Lagurus ovatus*	Sunray	*Helipterum*
Chrysanthemum	*Chrysanthemum*	Ivy	*Hedera*			Teasel	*Dipsacus fullonum*
Clubrush	*Scirpus*	Jonquil	*Narcissus*	Rat's tail statice	*Limonium suworowii = Psylliostachys suworowii*	Tobacco plant	*Nicotiana*
Cornflower	*Centaurea cyanus*	Lady's mantle	*Alchemilla*			Tulip	*Tulipa*
Daffodil	*Narcissus*	Larkspur	*Delphinium consolida*	Reed	*Phragmites australis*	Wheat	*Triticum*
Delphinium	*Delphinium*	Lilac	*Syringa*	Reed grass	*Phalaris arundinacea*	Yarrow	*Achillea*

SCIENTIFIC CLASSIFICATION: SECTION TWO

The following is an alphabetical list of the common names of plants
used in this section and their Latin equivalents.

Common name	Latin name
Acroclinium (sunray)	Acroclinium roseum – Helipterum roseum
Alyssum	Alyssum
Apple blossom	Malus sylvestris
Astrantia	Astrantia
Ash	Fraxinus excelsior
'Bachelor's Buttons' buttercup	Ranunculus aconitifolius
Bamboo	Arundinaria
Barley, black-eared	Hordeum
Beard grass	Polypogon
Bearded twitch grass	Agropyrom caninum
Beech	Fagus sylvatica
Bistort	Polygonum bistorta
Blackthorn	Prunus spinosa
'Blue Haze'	Acaena
Borage	Borago officinalis
Bottlebrush	Callistemon
Bracken fern	Pteridium aquilinum
Brome grass	Bromus commutatus
Buttercup	Ranunculus acris
Camomile	Matricaria matricariodes
Candytuft	Iberis umbellata
Carnation	Dianthus carophyllus
Carrot foliage	Daucus carota
Cherry blossom	Prunus sargentii
Chervil	Chaerophyllum temulentum
Chinese lantern	Physalis alkekengi
Clubrush	Scirpus
Cocksfoot grass (orchard grass)	Dactylis glomerata
Common bent grass	Agrostis tenuis
'Copper Carpet'	Acaena
Cornflower	Centaurea cyanus
Cow parsley	Anthriscus sylvestris
Cow parsnip	Heracleum sphondylium
Cowslip	Primula veris
Creeping bent grass	Agrostis stolonifera
Creeping cinquefoil	Potentilla reptans
Crested dog's tail grass	Cynosurus cristatus
Daisy	Bellis perennis
Delphinium	Delphinium elatum
Dogwood	Cornus alba spaethii
Elderberry	Sambucus nigra

Common name	Latin name
Euonymus	Euonymus japonicus
Fennel	Foeniculum vulgare
Feverfew	Chrysanthemum parthenium
Flowering currant	Ribes sanguineum
Fools' parsley	Aethusa cynapium
Forget-me-not	Myosotis
Fuchsia	Fuchsia magellanica
Geranium	Pelargonium
Glixia (grass daisy)	Aphyllanthes monspeliensis
Globe thistle	Echinops
Golden rod	Solidago
Greyhair grass	Corynephorus canescens
Guelder rose (cranberry bush)	Viburnum opulus
Gypsophila (baby's breath)	Gypsophila paniculata
Hairy tare vetch	Vicia hirsuta
Hare's or rabbit's tail grass	Lagurus ovatus
Hawthorn	Crataegus monogyna
Heart's ease (Johnny-jump-up)	Viola tricolor
Heather	Erica
Hebe	Hebe
Hedge bedstraw	Galium album
Hedge parsley	Torilis japonica
Honesty (silver dollar plant)	Lunaria annua
Hop trefoil	Trifolium campestre
Horseshoe vetch	Hippocrepis comosa
Hydrangea	Hydrangea
Japanese crab apple	Malus floribuna
Japanese maple	Acer palmatum
Knapweed	Centaurea nigra
Knotgrass	Polygonum aviculare
Lady's bedstraw	Galium verum
Lady's mantle	Alchemilla alpina and Alchemilla mollis
Larkspur	Delphinium consolida
Lavender	Lavandula angustifolia = L. spica or L. officinalis
Lobelia	Lobelia erinus
Loose silky bent grass	Apera spica-venti

Common name	Latin name
Lotus	Nelumbo lutea
Love-in-a-mist	Nigella damascena
Love-lies-bleeding	Amaranthus caudatus
Maidenhair fern	Adiantum pedatum
Maple	Acer campestre
Meadow fescue	Festuca pratensis
Meadowsweet	Filipendula ulmaria
Medick, yellow	Medicago
Melilot	Melilotus
Mind-your-own-business	Helxine soleirolii
Montbretia	Crocosmia rocosmiiflora
Mugwort	Artemisia vulgaris
Nipplewort (or broom bloom)	Laspana communis
Oats, wild	Avena fatua
Pansy	Viola
Pearl everlasting	Anaphalis
Peony	Paeonia lactiflora
Periwinkle	Vinca minor
Plumbago	Plumbago capensis
Polyanthus	Primula polyantha
Polypody fern	Polypodium
Poppy	Papaver
Potentilla (shrubby)	Potentilla fruticosa
Potentilla (woody)	Potentilla nepalensis
Primrose	Primula vulgaris
Quaking grass	Briza media and Briza maxima
Rat's tail statice	Limonium suworowii = Psylliostachys suworowii
Reed	Phragmites australis
Reed grass (also reed canary grass)	Phalaris arundinacea
Rhodanthe (sunray or Swan River everlasting)	Rhodanthe manglesii = Helipterum manglesii
Rice grass (cordgrass)	Spartina
Rock geranium	Geranium cinereum
Rock rose	Cistus
Rose	Rosa
Rose bay willow herb	Epilobium angustifolium
Rough meadow grass	Poa trivialis
Rue	Ruta graveolens

Common name	Latin name
Russian vine (silver lace vine)	Polygonum aubertii
Rye grass	Lolium perenne
Salad burnet	Sanguisorba minor
Sandflower (winged everlasting)	Ammobium alatum
Saxifrage	Saxifraga moschata
Sea holly	Eryngium oliverianum
Sea lavender	Limonium tataricum = Goniolimon tataricum
Shepherd's purse	Capella bursa-pastoris
Silverweed	Potentilla anserina
Smoke bush (smoketree)	Cotinus coggygria
Snowdrop	Galanthus nivalis
'Sol d'Or'	Narcissus tazetta
Speedwell	Veronica officinalis
Spiraea (spring flowering)	Spiraea 'Arguta'
Spiraea (summer flowering)	Spiraea bumalda
Squirrel tailed fescue	Festuca bromides
Star of Bethlehem	Ornithogalum umbellatum
Statice	Limonium sinuatum
Strawflower or everlasting	Helichrysum
Sumach	Rhus typhina
Sunray	Helipterum
Sweet cicely	Myrrhis odorata
Thyme	Thymus serpyllum
Traveller's joy	Clematis vitalba
Tufted hair grass	Deschampsia cespitosa
Verbena	Verbena hybrida
Vetch	Vicia sativa
Virginia creeper	Parthenocissus quinquefolia
Wayfaring tree	Viburnum lantana
Whitebeam	Sorbus aria
Wild carrot (Queen Ann's lace)	Daucus carota
Wild strawberry	Fragaria vesca
Willow	Salix
Wood avens (clove root)	Geum urbanum
Yarrow	Achillea

DRYING METHODS

Suitable Plants for Preserving in Desiccants

Anemone	Hellibore
Bells of Ireland	Hollyhock
Buttercup	Larkspur
Camellia	Lily flowerheads
Cornflower	Marigold
Daffodil	Mimosa
Dahlia	Monkshood
Daisy	Orchid
Delphinium	Paeony
Elderberry	Pansy
Forget-me-not	Primrose
Freesia	Ranunculus
Gentian	Rose
Geranium	Violet

Suitable Plants for Preserving in Glycerine

Aspidistra leaves	Ivy leaves
Barley	Lady's mantle
Beech leaves	Laurel leaves
Bells of Ireland	Magnolia leaves
Box leaves	Mahonia leaves
Bracken fern	Oak leaves
Chestnut leaves	Oats
Eucalyptus leaves	Old man's beard
Hawthorn leaves	Quaking grass
Holly leaves	Rabbit's or hare's tail grass
Hops	Wheat
Hydrangea	

Suitable Plants for Air Drying

Acanthus	Eucalyptus leaves	Iris seedheads	Protea
Acroclinium	Gladioli seedheads	Lady's mantle	Rhodanthe
Anaphalis	Globe thistle seedheads	Larkspur	Rose
Bamboo	Golden rod	Lavender	Sea holly
Barley	Grasses	Lotus seedheads	Sea lavender
Bells of Ireland	Gypsophila	Love-in-a-mist	Shepherd's purse
Bottlebrush	Heather	Lupin seedheads	Statice
Chinese lantern	Helichrysum	Mimosa	Sunray
Clary	Hogweed seedheads	Monkshood	Sweetcorn
Cornflower	Hollyhock seedheads	Moss	Teasel seedheads
Cow parsley seedheads	Honesty seedheads	Oats	Thistle seedheads
Delphinium	Hops	Onion seedheads	Wheat
Dock	Hydrangea	Poppy seedheads	Xeranthemum

DRIED & PRESSED FLOWERS

INTRODUCTION

Today, dried and pressed flower arranging is a popular
and relaxing pastime, associated with designs as packed with
colour and variety as any fresh flower arrangement. And the displays
are there to be enjoyed for years rather than merely days. The designs
featured in this section range from garlands, wreaths, mobiles, pomanders
and centrepieces — all made using dried flowers — to pictures,
greeting cards, paperweights and many more novelty ideas
made with a beautiful array of pressed flowers.

This section will guide you through all stages of both hobbies,
from growing and drying the flowers to creating the finished design.
Detailed introductions to both crafts contain information on the various
techniques involved, such as how to dry the flowers and wire them into bunches,
or make a press and fix the flowers in an arrangement. There are two beautiful colour
plates illustrating some of the more commonly-used plants. Except in those cases
where the Latin name is more often used, most plants have been given their
common names (with alternative common names appearing in brackets).
The scientific names of plants have also been given on page 95.

DRIED FLOWERS

In recent years the popularity of dried flowers has soared as the variety and availability of plant material has increased one-hundred-fold. Whereas twenty years ago choice was restricted to a few common flowers and grasses, such as pampas grass, helichrysum (strawflowers or everlasting) and limonium (statice and sea lavender), today a host of specialist shops are bursting with exciting and colourful flowers from all over the world — plants such as proteas, dryandras and leucodendrons.

BUYING DRIED FLOWERS

When buying dried flowers, the wide range of plants now available may at first seem confusing. The beginner might be well advised to start by purchasing mixed bunches which can usually be bought in large department stores, gift shops and some fresh flower shops. But for real variety, it is best to buy individual bunches from a specialist shop. Often, only three or four varieties are all you need to create a colourful and imaginative display.

Decide what colours you want first, either choosing complementary colours such as yellows and oranges, reds and pinks, blues and purples or picking strikingly contrasting colours — yellows and purples, reds and blues, pinks and oranges. Think also about tonal contrast in your arrangement: white and yellow add welcome highlights to dark displays; dark browns or greens give depth to bright arrangements.

Shape and texture are also very important when planning a display; unusual shapes and contrasting textures add interest and can prevent an arrangement from looking uninspired. The illustration below shows some of the unusual things you can add to your designs, including nuts, cones, fungi, twigs, spices and coral. Ribbons and fabric can also add colour and interest. So when gathering materials for your arrangements, try looking further than your local florist.

GROWING YOUR OWN

Growing your own flowers is by far the cheapest way of pursuing this hobby and has the advantage of providing you with colour in the garden as well as inside the home. Plants should be picked on a dry day just before the flowers are fully open, and preferably in the middle of the day when the sap is rising. If the flowers you pick are wet from rain or dew, before you preserve them, gently shake them and leave the stems standing in some shallow water until the petals are dry.

One of the easiest methods of drying flowers is to hang them upside down in a warm, dark, airy place; this helps to preserve the flowers' natural colour. Not all plants are suitable for drying this way though — others are better preserved using desiccants or glycerine. Drying methods are discussed in more detail opposite.

To avoid leaving large bare patches in your garden after you have gathered the flowers, intersperse the flowers amongst other plants when planting so that their loss is not so noticeable later on. Suitable plants to grow for drying include everlastings such as helichrysum, helipterum, xeranthemum and eryngium (sea holly), plus heather, limonium, larkspur, golden rod, yarrow, lavender, lady's mantle, allium and poppy. Dried roses are beautiful, but multi-petalled varieties are more suitable for preserving than single-petalled ones.

A wide range of materials can be used to add interest to arrangements. Shown left are: 1) pot-pourri; 2) lotus seedheads; 3) repens rosette; 4) platyspernum cones; 5) Leucodendron plumosum; 6) walnuts; 7) coral; 8) sponge mushroom; 9) lagenaria fruit; 10) gourds; 11) artificial berries; 12) willow branch; 13) tallscreen; 14) lomius; 15) cinnamon sticks; 16) Spanish root; 17) cones.

Flowers such as statice, larkspur and pearl achillea can be air dried. Hang them in small bunches, binding the stems first with rubber (elastic) bands.

Also consider growing grasses, ferns and bracken for contrast in your arrangements. Foliage is also important: beech, holly, ivy, bay, hornbeam and lime (linden) are all good for preserving.

If you don't have a garden, pot plants can be a source of material. And keep an eye open on country walks; gather cones, bark, nuts and interestingly shaped twigs from woodlands; wild flowers from meadows, hedgerows and roadsides. Try experimenting with as many plants as you can to see if they are suitable for drying.

DRYING METHODS

There are a number of different ways of drying flowers and foliage and on page 95 you will find a table listing various plants and their methods of preservation. One of the easiest methods is air drying. A number of flowers (particularly the everlastings) can simply be left hanging upside down to dry in a warm, dark, airy place such as an airing cupboard, attic, loft or garage. It is important that the flowers are not put in direct sunlight as this will cause their colours to fade. Bind the flowers together into bunches before hanging them. Rubber bands are best for this purpose because the flower stems will shrink as they dry. Alternatively, use raffia, pipe cleaners or gardeners' string, being sure to tighten it around the stems regularly.

Suspend the flowers from a pole or some rope and leave them till they are dry and crisp to the touch. Make sure that the stems are completely dry, particularly at the top, otherwise the heads will soon droop. The drying time varies according to the conditions and type of plant, but it usually takes from one to four weeks.

Some plants, such as sea lavender and pampas grass, dry best standing upright in a jam jar or vase. Sand can be used to weight the jar and support the stems. Other plants should be placed in shallow water — about 5cm (2in) deep — to dry. Hydrangea and gypsophila dry best this way. Most grasses, fungi and twigs should be dried flat on an absorbent surface such as cardboard or newspaper. Leaves dried this way tend to shrivel but do retain their natural colour. To prevent the seeds falling off grasses and cereals, and to give added strength to their stems, spray the plants with hair spray before, or even after, drying.

DESICCANTS

Desiccants — or drying agents — draw moisture from the plants and help to preserve the natural colours and form of flowers. One of the simplest to use — though not the cheapest — is silica gel, which can be bought from most hardware stores. It usually comes in the form of white crystals which should be ground down to a finer grade before using. (Blue indicator crystals are also available — these turn pink when they have absorbed water.) Put a layer of crystals into the base of an air-tight container and place several wired flowerheads on top. Using a spoon, carefully cover the flowers with more of the desiccant, making sure that the crystals fall between the petals but do not misshape them. When the flowers are fully covered close the container and leave for a couple of days.

Borax is less expensive than silica gel, though it takes longer to work — at least ten days. Ideally it should be mixed with dry silver sand: three parts borax to two parts sand. Cover the flowers as with the silica gel.

GLYCERINE

A mixture of one part glycerine to two parts warm water is ideal for preserving the shape and suppleness of foliage. Either fully submerge the leaves in the solution (singly or in small sprays) or stand the stems of larger sprays in about 8-10cm (3-4in) of mixture. Cut the stems at a sharp angle and hammer the ends of woody stems to aid absorption. Gradually the glycerine will replace the water in the leaves. Submerged leaves take about two days, whereas plants left standing in the mixture take up to four weeks to dry; start checking after the first week.

Foliage, such as copper beech, can be preserved in a mixture of glycerine and water. This method stops the leaves from becoming brittle and misshapen.

Silica gel is used to preserve the shape and colour of roses. Carefully cover the flower with finely-ground crystals, being sure not to crush the petals.

The picture below shows a range of equipment used in dried flower arranging. Certain items may only be required occasionally, as the need arises — wreath wrap for example is only used when making moss wreaths and garlands — whereas other items are considered essential; no flower arranger could cope for long without a strong pair of florists' scissors, a sharp knife, some wire and blocks of florists' foam.

THE MECHANICS

The various items used to support the flowers in an arrangement are known as the mechanics. Florists' foam is the most popular mechanic. It comes in two forms: one for fresh flower arrangements (designed to absorb and hold water), the other for dried arrangements. The latter, often referred to as dry foam, comes in several shapes and sizes — spheres, blocks and cones — and can easily be cut down to any size or shape to fit a container.

Another much-used mechanic is wire mesh which is particularly good for larger, heavier arrangements. It can either be crumpled into a ball or other shape to fit inside the container or it can be packed with moss to form a more solid base. This latter method is sometimes used for making garlands and wreaths.

SECURING THE MECHANICS

It is sometimes possible to wedge the foam or wire mesh into a container so that it is held firm. But usually you will need to secure it in position. Florists' tape is very useful for attaching foam to the base of a container or, where necessary, for holding two or more pieces of foam together.

Small plastic pinholders are also available for securing foam; they can be stuck down on to the container using fixative and the foam can then be pushed firmly on to the pins. Wire is used for attaching both foam and wire mesh to containers — particularly baskets where the wire can be threaded through the wicker work and the ends twisted together to secure firmly in place.

Plaster of Paris is sometimes used in dried flower arranging to weight top heavy displays or support the mechanics — for example, when making a floral tree (see page 118).

Glue is sometimes used for sticking dry foam on to a container. It is also useful for sticking plant materials together or gluing flowerheads or small posies on to a base, such as a box or a picture frame.

WIRE AND STRING

A variety of wire is used in dried flower arranging. Stub wires are straight lengths of wire that are generally used for supporting single flowerheads or binding together small groups of flowers (see opposite). They are also used for supporting more unusual objects in an arrangement such as nuts, cones and so forth. The wires come in a range of different thicknesses, or gauges. Black reel wire is used for making moss wreaths and garlands, as these require a continuous length of wire (see page 106). You can also buy reels of fine silver florists' wire (sometimes called rose wire) which is used for more delicate work, for example, for binding dried flowers together into posies (see page 135) or, in conjunction with string, for making small garlands (see page 145). Rose wire also comes in short lengths, about 15cm (6in) long. This can be used for binding miniature posies or wiring ribbon bows (see opposite).

The equipment used in dried flower arranging includes: 1) plaster of Paris; 2) dry foam; 3) a sharp knife; 4) strong florists' scissors; 5) wreath wrap; 6) string; 7) florists' tape; 8) fixative; 9) glue; 10) plastic pinholders; 11) fine silver reel (rose) wire 12) black reel wire; 13) 15cm (6in) fine silver (rose) wire; 14, 15, and 16) stub wires; 17) wire mesh.

CUTTING IMPLEMENTS

A strong pair of florists' scissors is essential for cutting plants down to size. Some scissors have a special wire-cutting edge; if yours do not, you will also require wire-cutters. Secateurs (pruning shears) are useful for woody stems. A sharp knife is needed for stripping off unwanted leaves and branches from stems, and a second, longer knife is useful for slicing up large blocks of florists' foam.

BASIC TECHNIQUES

Some dried flowers — yarrow and larkspur for example — have strong, firm stems that need no support. Others, such as helichrysums, have weak stems that cannot withstand the weight of the flowerheads. In the latter case, wire can be used to support the flower. Cut a stem down to about 4cm (1½in) and place it against one end of a stub wire. Then bind the length of the stem to the wire using silver reel wire. (If you like, you can then cover the new 'stem' by binding florists' gutta-percha tape around both the plant stem and the stub wire.) This method can also be used for lengthening stems that are too short. For hollow-stemmed plants, such as safflowers and amaranthus, simply push a length of stub wire into the hollow end of the stem.

To increase the impact of colours in a display, flowers are frequently tied into small bunches before they are arranged. To do this, cut down the stems of two or three flowers — weak stems should be cut down to about 4cm (1½in); strong ones can be left longer. Take a length of stub wire and bend back the top 3-4cm (1-1½in) to form a hair-pin shape. Place the pin against the end of the stems, bent end towards the flowerheads. Then, starting about half way down the pin, begin to wind the long end of the wire around both the stems and the short end of the wire. Bind it about three times as shown below, then straighten it so that it forms a 'stem'. Trim the wire to the required length and insert it into the display.

Bows are frequently used to decorate dried flower arrangements. The easiest way to make a perfect bow is to wire it as described right. Other techniques used in dried flower arranging, such as making a garland or wreath, are described on page 106.

To give flowers more impact in a display, wire them into small bunches before arranging them. First bend the end of a stub wire to form a hair-pin shape.

Cut the flower stems short and place them against the pin. Wind the long end of wire round about three times then straighten it to make a 'stem'.

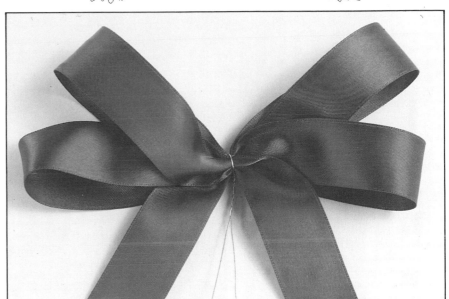

Bows are often used to put the finishing touches to an arrangement. To make this double bow, take a length of satin ribbon about 60cm (2ft) long and make a loop at one end. Form a second loop as shown to make a bow shape. Ensure each time you loop the ribbon that you keep it right side out.

Loop the long tail over the front of the bow to form a third loop, and then to the back to make a fourth loop as shown.

Wrap a length of rose wire round the centre of the bow and secure it by twisting the ends together. Use the ends of the wire to attach the bow to the arrangement. Now simply trim the tails to the required length, cutting them in a V-shape to finish off. This technique can easily be adapted to make a single bow or even a triple or quadruple one.

MAKING A GARLAND

There are several ways of making a garland; this is but one of them. Another method is shown on page 128. Begin by taking some fresh, damp sphagnum moss. Knead it to get rid of any large lumps, then roll it into a long cylindrical shape. Don't make the roll too thick as the flowers will eventually fatten it up.

Starting at one end, bind black reel wire tightly round the moss roll, keeping the turns quite close together. Trim off any straggly pieces of moss as you go.

Allow the garland to dry before inserting the flowers. These should be wired in small bunches and inserted at an acute angle into the moss rather than at right angles. A variation on this method, often used for larger garlands, is to roll the moss out on top of a length of wire mesh. You then roll the moss up in the mesh and turn the raw edges of wire under to secure it.

MAKING A WREATH

To make a wreath such as this you need a wire wreath frame and some dry sphagnum moss. Knead the moss to get rid of any lumps then pack a handful into the frame.

Attach some black reel wire to the frame and, working in an anti-clockwise direction, begin to bind the moss-filled frame, pulling tightly with each turn. Continue to pack and bind the moss into the frame until the whole wreath is complete.

If you like, you can cover the ring with plastic wreath wrap. Attach one end of the wrap to the ring using a wire pin then wind the wrap around the wreath as shown. Wire the flowers into small bunches and insert them into the wreath. Another way to make a wreath is to create a garland as described left: then bend it into a ring and secure the ends with wire.

Helichrysum
(Strawflower or everlasting)

Solidago
(Golden rod)

Acroclinium
(also Helipterum — sunray)

Physalis
(Chinese lantern)

Papaver
(Poppy seedheads)

Rosa
(Rose)

Helichrysum
(South African daisy)

Achillea
(Lonas — a type of yarrow)

Amaranthus
(Love-lies-bleeding)

Lagarus
(Rabbit's or hare's tail grass)

Lunaria
(Honesty)

Xeranthemum

Delphinium
(Larkspur)

Limonium sinuatum
(Statice)

Phalaris
(Reed grass)

Lavandula
(Lavender)

Hydrangea

Hordeum
(Black-eared barley)

Avena fatua
(Wild oats)

Limonium (Goniolimon) tataricum
(Sea lavender)

An old bicycle basket makes the perfect container for this delightfully random display of flowers. First, fill the top of the basket with wire mesh, attaching it to the sides with reel wire threaded through the wicker. Now begin to build up the outline using tall stems of blue larkspur. Fill in the shape using fluffy white gypsophila (baby's breath).

In this attractive design, contrasting colours and textures combine to create a delightful picture. Take a small wicker basket and fill it with wire mesh, attaching the mesh at intervals to the side of the basket with wire. A brightly coloured basket such as this one looks particularly effective. Start to build up the outline of the display using single lengths of blue larkspur.

Complete the outline with wired bunches of sea holly, keeping the shape full and wide. Next, fill in with bunches of large pink helichrysum (strawflower or everlasting). Keep them shorter than the other plants so that they lie lower down in the arrangement.

Finally, pick out the colour of the basket with bunches of bright pink rabbit's or hare's tail grass, scattering them throughout the arrangement and bringing it to life.

Next, position clumps of flowering love-in-a-mist lower down in the arrangement, keeping them well scattered. The focal flowers in the display are pretty pink and yellow acroclinium (sunray). Arrange large clumps of them throughout, keeping the heads well exposed. Finish off with a ring of hydrangea around the rim of the basket.

Acombination of lavender and red helichrysum form a delightful surround for this small basket of pot-pourri. Begin by wiring small bunches of lavender — about three to four stems each. Attach a bunch to the rim of the basket by wrapping the wire through the wicker work. Position the next bunch over the stems of the first to cover the wires. Continue round the rim.

The same basket as the one used opposite but a completely different design — here, netting has been used to create a soft billowing effect. Wire together clumps of red amaranthus (love-lies-bleeding) and insert them at intervals around the rim of the basket. Keep the angles irregular so that some stems are standing up, others hanging down.

When the rim is fully covered, cover the handle in the same way. Add a splash of colour to the display with wired bunches of small red helichrysum (everlasting or strawflower). Attach them at intervals to the rim of the basket, using the same method as before. Put two more bunches on the handle.

Fill in with clumps of blue larkspur and soft pink *Helichrysum casianum,* forming a dense ring of flowers around the basket.

Make a single bow out of deep red ribbon, wiring it together as described on page 105. Attach the bow to the middle of the handle and cover the wire with a strand of lavender; fix this in place using fine silver rose wire. To finish, fill the basket with pot-pourri, choosing a type that complements the colours of the arrangement.

Take three strips of lilac netting and form single bows, wiring them as described on page 105. Attach bows to the base of the handle on either side and put the third one in the middle as shown. Finally, fill the basket with sweet-smelling pot-pourri.

Bring a touch of the country into your living room with this beautiful array of garden flowers. Take a wicker shopping basket and fill the top with wire mesh, attaching the mesh to the sides of the basket with wire. Form a base for the arrangement by packing the mesh with wired bunches of sea lavender.

Wire clumps of love-in-a-mist and insert them into the arrangement so that they stand out above the sea lavender. Then start to fill in with bunches of soft pink larkspur. Try to keep the arrangement slightly parted around the handle so that the latter is not totally obscured. Finish filling in with bunches of lady's mantle, then add several garden roses to complete the picture.

A classic willow pattern vegetable dish serves up an exciting Oriental display of flowers and curling tallscreen. Begin by cutting a block of florists' foam to fit inside the dish. Secure the foam with florists' tape as shown. Prop the lid up against the dish, leaving three quarters of the foam exposed.

Start to build up the general shape of the arrangement using wired clumps of helichrysum (strawflower or everlasting). Then fill in with large bunches of yarrow, covering most of the foam. Keep the shape low and within the outline of the dish.

Add a complete contrast of colour and texture with several stems of tallscreen — their fascinating shape adds interest to any arrangement. Place them at various angles, keeping them taller than the other plants so that they are clearly visible.

Finish off with a few stems of flowering love-in-a-mist, arranging them so that they break out of the general, low-lying outline. The faint hint of blue in these flowers picks up the blue in the dish.

Abeautiful old tobacco pot makes a perfect setting for a striking display of brightly coloured flowers. Note how the blue and orange in the china have been picked up by the colours of the flowers. First, cut a block of florists' foam to fit snugly inside the pot.

Using wired bunches of helichrysum (strawflower or everlasting), build up a dome shape to reflect the shape of the pot. Then add clusters of blue-dyed *Leucodendron brunia*. The unusual shape of this plant will always add interest to any arrangement.

Finally, add clumps of bright yellow morrison to fill in any gaps and complete the display.

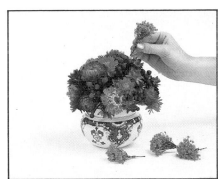

Agiant Minton cup and saucer doubles up as a pot-pourri container. The same effect can easily be created with a normal-sized cup and saucer, using smaller-headed flowers. Make a cylinder out of wire mesh and bend it into a ring large enough to fit around the base of the cup. Knot the ends of the wire together.

Wire several bunches of deep pink helichrysum (strawflower or everlasting), blue-dyed cluster-flowered sunray and creamy cauliflower. Slot them alternately into the mesh, packing them in tightly to cover the wire but being sure not to obscure the pattern on the side of the cup.

Once the 'garland' has been completed, you can fill the cup with pot-pourri, choosing a mixture that complements the colours of the arrangement.

A beautiful old china jug, bursting with sheaves of oats, makes a striking arrangement for the hallway. Begin by making a garland of flowers to fit round the neck of the jug. Construct the frame of the garland using sphagnum moss and reel wire, following the instructions given in detail on page 106. Leave long tails of wire at either end of the garland.

When the frame is completed, mould a piece of wire mesh into a ball and put it into the jug.

Wrap the moss frame round the neck of the jug and secure it in position by twisting the free ends of the wire together. Select some flowers that co-ordinate with the colours in the jug. Used here are pale blue helichrysum (strawflower or everlasting), blue-dyed achillea and pearl achillea (two types of yarrow).

Wire the flowers into small bunches and insert them into the garland, pushing the wires in at a slight angle rather than at right angles. Arrange the different types alternately, packing them close together to form a thick ring of flowers all the way round the jug.

To complete the display, cut a large amount of oats down to the same height and push them, a bundle at a time, into the wire mesh ball at the base of the jug. Make sure they are packed very tightly and stand straight.

Arrange clumps of sea holly next, sprinkling them throughout. They add an interesting hint of blue to the neutral tones of the arrangement. Now add a dramatic contrast in shape and texture with some large globe thistle heads. Concentrate these around the handle, pushing some deep into the arrangement, and then place a few long stems in the foreground.

This wild arrangement is designed to look like a freshly-gathered basket of flowers and grasses. Use a basket with a low 'lip' at one end and put a ball of wire mesh at the taller end; secure it with wire. Now arrange several large clumps of oats, keeping those at the front long so that they overhang the lip, those further back becoming shorter and more upright.

Now intersperse the oats with wired bunches of love-in-a-mist, maintaining the general shape, with long low-lying stems at the front, shorter upright ones at the back. Follow these with bunches of small poppy seedheads, arranged mainly towards the front of the display so that they appear to be spilling out over the lip. Add a few larger poppy seedheads as well for contrast.

Soften the whole arrangement by adding a few grasses and then finish off by placing several lotus seedheads at the back, using them to cover any exposed wire mesh.

Bring an old frame to life with this attractive arrangement of oats and flowers. Cut four lengths of wire mesh, making them slightly longer than the sides of the frame. Roll them up into tubes about 3cm (1in) in diameter and fix them tightly round the frame, joining them at the corners with wire.

This attractive design illustrates how much a floral arrangement can enhance a plain picture frame — it's easy to do but so very effective. Cut a slice of florists' foam to fit one corner of the frame and tape it in place. Begin to loosely build up the shape using single stems of clubrush.

Wire large clumps of oats and pack them tightly into the wire mesh frame so that the strands become entangled and hold each other together. The oats provide a good base for the other plants and help to keep them in place. Now add wired bunches of yellow anaphalis (pearl everlasting), arranging them at intervals around the frame.

Add a splash of colour throughout the display with bright yellow cressia, allowing some to trail across the frame and picture. Then insert a number of single stems of bottlebrush to add interest and colour.

Position wired bunches of pink *Helichrysum casianum* in amongst the oats, keeping them close to the anaphalis. Finish off with several groups of blue *Leucodendron brunia*, their rich, dark colour adding contrast to the arrangement.

Fill out the display with plenty of bottlebrush foliage. Then add highlights with a few white leaf skeletons such as these peepal leaves.

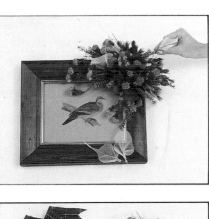

Finally, make a double bow out of tartan ribbon, following the instructions on page 105. Attach this to the lower portion of the arrangement so that the long tails of the bow trail across the frame. Repeat the whole procedure on the opposite corner, being sure to keep the design well balanced.

Next, make a ring of wire mesh, slightly deeper than the container and wide enough to fit snuggly round it. The ring must be double thickness so you can pack it with dry sphagnum moss. When it is fully packed, neatly bend the raw edges of wire over to close the ring. Now cut several equal lengths of birch twigs and attach them to the moss ring using wire pins — two per twig.

Cover the wire pins by tying long strands of raffia around the ring. Once the plaster has set, place the container inside the wire surround. Take a large sphere of florists' foam and scrape out the centre using a knife. Press the ball on to the wooden 'stem' of the tree, making sure it is held firm. Now wire some small bunches of flowers, leaving at least 3cm (1in) of wire 'tail'.

The flowers used here are orange and yellow helichrysum (strawflower or everlasting), blue larkspur and green amaranthus (love-lies-bleeding). Use the helichrysum first to form the shape, keeping the arrangement spherical. Next add the larkspur and amaranthus, making sure they do not protrude too far out of the arrangement and break up the shape.

This ever-popular form of floral arrangement is not as difficult to achieve as you might think. Begin by selecting a suitable container for the base. Mix up some plaster of Paris with water and fill the container. Quickly insert an interestingly-shaped branch for the stem, holding it in position for a couple of minutes until the plaster begins to set.

Finish off by putting pieces of moss around the base of the tree to hide the plaster of Paris and the wire mesh.

This unusual and imaginative wreath makes a striking decoration to hang on the door during the winter. To create it, you will first need to buy a twig wreath from your local florist. Begin the arrangement by wiring small bunches of oak leaves together. Also take a few pieces of sponge mushroom and push wires through one side.

Attach the leaves and fungus to the wreath, forming three groups evenly spaced around the ring. Now wire up some lotus seedheads — wiring the large ones singly and the small ones in groups of two or three. Insert these in amongst the other plants.

Push short lengths of wire as far as they will go through one end of some walnuts. Form small groups of about three to four nuts each by twisting the wires together. Slot the walnuts into the three groups of plants. Next add a few witch hazel twigs, allowing them to break out of the arrangement and cover some bare patches between the groups.

To finish, wire together several bunches of yarrow and slot them into the arrangement, using them to close up the gaps slightly between the three main groups. The yarrow adds necessary colour to the wreath and brings it to life.

A attractive winter's wreath in muted creams and golds makes a pleasant change from the usual seasonal reds and greens, and gives a different and stylish Christmas decoration. Begin by covering a wreath ring in sphagnum moss, as shown in more detail on page 106.

Wire together some clumps of cream sea lavender and virtually cover the entire ring with it. Next, take some purple statice and wire together several bunches.

Co-ordinate a floral display with your curtains or soft furnishings by covering the base in some matching fabric. Take a piece of left-over material and wrap it round a suitable basket. Pack the inside of the basket with wire mesh and hold it in place using strips of wire pushed through both the fabric and the wicker work.

Intersperse the purple statice evenly amongst the cream coloured flowers which form the base of the garland. Then, place at regular intervals some wired clumps of yarrow and rhodanthe (sunray).

Wire bunches of beige cluster-flowered sunray and bright yellow yarrow and pack them tightly into the wire mesh, forming a dome-shaped outline. Now scatter several wired bunches of reed grass throughout the arrangement.

Finally, gather about 10 to 12 cones and wire them together in a large bunch. With more wire fix the cones to the wreath at the front. Pull a few strands of the flowers between the cones to add contrast. Intersperse a few more cones throughout the wreath as shown to complete the picture. This combination of flowers and cones is remarkably inexpensive, yet the result is quite stunning.

Add large wired bunches of lavender next, keeping the stems long so that the flowers stand out above the other plants. Finish off with groups of South African daisies (a type of helichrysum). These plants have been chosen to match the colours in the fabric so, when you follow this design, alter the range of flowers according to your colour scheme.

This stunning wreath, with its wealth of contrasting colours and materials, makes a beautiful decoration to hang on the door at any time of the year. Begin by making a base (following the instructions given in full on page 106) using a wire frame and some sphagnum moss. Cover the base with green wreath wrap.

Take some colourful fabric and cut it up into rectangles. Now wrap about 8 to 10 small foam spheres in the fabric, gathering the material at the top and securing with wire. Leave long wire 'tails' for attaching the balls to the frame. Position the spheres in groups of two or three at regular intervals around the wreath.

Wire clumps of green amaranthus (love-lies-bleeding) and insert them into the wreath, keeping them generally quite close to the fabric spheres.

Next, wire clumps of white larkspur and intersperse these amongst the amaranthus. These reflect the white in the fabric and add highlights to the arrangement. Wire together several groups of cones and place them standing upright in the arrangement so that they do not get lost among the other plants.

Soften the display by scattering bunches of soft pink rabbit's or hare's tail grass throughout. The seeds tend to moult very easily so be careful when wiring and inserting the grass not to overhandle it.

Pick out the colours in the fabric by dotting clumps of rust coloured nipplewort (or broom bloom) throughout. The dark tones will also add depth to the display.

Finish off with a few colourful satin bows. You can either make double bows (as described on page 105) or single ones as shown here. Insert the bows in amongst the fabric spheres, trailing the tails prettily over the arrangement.

For the celebration of any Scottish event, such as Burns' night (January 26th), create this striking tartan wreath. First you will need to buy a twig ring from a florist. Begin the garland by individually wiring several heads of red rose. Arrange these in three small groups, evenly spaced around the ring.

Next, wire together nine small bunches of anaphalis (pearl everlasting) and push them into the ring so that they surround the roses. Take three lengths of tartan ribbon and make three single bows (following the instructions on page 105).

Take a fourth piece of ribbon, fold it in half and push a piece of wire through the folded end: this will form the long 'tails' of the arrangement. Cut a 'V' shape in the ends of the ribbons to finish them neatly, then wire a bow into each of the three gaps between the flowers. To complete the picture, wire the tartan tails beneath one of the bows.

T his beautiful design makes the perfect decoration for Valentine's day. Take some dry, bendy silver birch twigs, trim off all the rough ends and divide them into two equal bundles, about 60cm (24in) long. Join the two bundles at one end with stub wires; and again about 20cm (8in) further along. Now bend either side round to form a heart shape as shown.

Bind the three ends firmly with wire, then wrap wire around four other points on the heart to hold the twigs together. Cover each of the wired areas with red satin or gift wrap ribbon, gluing each strip in place at the back. Wire up a couple of red bows (as described on page 105) and put one on either side of the heart.

Attach a length of wired ribbon to the top of the heart for hanging. To soften the effect, take small clumps of gypsophila (baby's breath) and push them in between the ribbon bands and the twigs. To finish off, mix some more gypsophila with some tiny red spray roses and position them at the base of the heart.

A collection of brilliantly coloured flowers makes a striking display for the sideboard. Begin by moulding some wire mesh into a three-dimensional shape, keeping the base flat and the top end open. Pack the mesh with dry sphagnum moss, then close up the open end. Now insert wired bunches of stirlingia — tall, upright stems at the top, shorter, horizontal ones lower down.

Next, arrange a few stems of blue larkspur around the top, and shorter bunches of blue statice lower down, following the general pattern set by the stirlingia. Follow with wired bunches of pink-dyed quaking grass, breaking out of the outline, and a few clumps of blue-dyed *Leucodendron brunia*.

Once you are happy with the general shape of the arrangement, start to fill in with bunches of large pink helichrysum (strawflower or everlasting). Pack them deep into the display. Add bright yellow highlights next with bunches of cluster-flowered helichrysum.

Finally, wire together a few bunches of rich red roses and scatter them throughout the display. It is important to position the roses last, because this ensures that the heads remain well exposed.

A couple of old wooden spoons form the basis of a pretty arrangement that would brighten up any kitchen. First, wire the spoons together at an angle as shown, winding the wire round the handles several times to secure firmly.

Wire together several small groups of plants, choosing an attractive range of colours. Shown here is yellow quaking grass, white helichrysum (strawflower or everlasting) and dudinea seedheads. Wire the small groups together to form one large bunch and attach this to the spoons so that the blooms sit prettily over the bowls.

Make a large bright double bow out of satin ribbon, following the instructions on page 105, and tie it with a second length of ribbon around the spoons and the posy.

A pair of butter pats makes an unusual setting for this kitchen design. Take a length of ribbon and wire up one end. Thread the ribbon through both holes from the front, leaving a long tail between the pats. Loop the ribbon over the top and thread through from the front again, pulling it tight. Make a second loop in the same way, leaving it long for hanging the display.

Secure the wired end of ribbon at the back with a knot; cut off any excess. Wire a small bow on to the front of the pats. Then attach half a sphere of florists' foam to the ribbon 'tail' using tape. Wire small bunches of blue jasilda and tiny red helichrysum and push them into the ball, packing them tightly together.

Add longer stems of blue larkspur, leaving some pieces trailing down the pats to break up the outline of the ball. Finally, wire up short double loops of ribbon and intersperse them among the flowers, finishing off with a couple of longer strands at the bottom.

The framework of this seasonal garland is made of cones and walnuts. Wire the cones by wrapping stub wire around the base. For the walnuts, push stub wire through one end as far as it will go. Take a group of cones and nuts and twist the wires together. Add to the base of the group and twist the wires again to secure. Continue in this way until the garland is long enough.

Make a double bow out of gold gift wrap ribbon (following the instructions on page 105) and wire two extra tails on to it. (Just fold a length of ribbon in half for the tails and wire in the middle.) Attach the bow to one end of the garland, then wire a long length of ribbon to the same end. Wrap this through the garland, twisting it round the cones. Leave a long tail at the far end.

To finish, wire together small groups of bright Chinese lanterns and bunches of quaking grass. Intersperse them amongst the cones, entangling the wires to secure them.

Not as sweet smelling perhaps as some of the other arrangements, but certainly very useful. First make a tied bunch of flowers as follows. Bind a small group of flowers with a length of reel wire. Gradually add more flowers to the bunch, binding them with the same length of wire, until the posy is the desired size.

The flowers used here are rat's tail statice and dryandra. Tie a length of raffia round the end of the posy and finish off with a bow. Wire the posy on to the end of a purchased garland of garlic bulbs. Complete the picture by wiring about five large protea heads and binding them on to the garland in amongst the garlic.

An old cotton spool is transformed by a lively display of bright yellow flowers. Make a garland of flowers as follows. Attach some reel wire to a length of string, about 20cm (8in) from one end. Position a small group of flowers against the join and wrap the wire round the stems to secure. Put another group of flowers over the stems of the first and secure as before.

Continue in this way until the garland is long enough to go round the spool. The flowers used here are brilliant yellow helichrysum (strawflower or everlasting), white larkspur and fluffy golden morrison. Attach the garland to the base of the spool by tying the string round it. Wrap the garland round the spool and secure at the top with the other end of the string.

Don't throw away that old broken flower pot — transform it instead into a stunning autumnal arrangement using black-eared barley and bright yellow helichrysum (strawflower or everlasting). Wedge a piece of florists' foam into the broken pot and secure it with tape. Now build up the shape of the arrangement with the barley, putting the discarded stems to one side.

Place longer stems of barley into the base of the display and generally shorter ones at the top, around the rim. Intersperse the barley with cluster-flowered helichrysum, placing the heads deep in the arrangement. Concentrate the yellow around the rim of the pot to cover up any foam still visible.

Run a line of helichrysum around the broken edge of the pot, pushing the stems into the foam or gluing the heads on if necessary. Finally, take the discarded barley stems and cut off the ends at a sharp angle. Now position them at the back of the display, splaying them out so that they appear to be continuous with the stems at the front.

W ood always provides a perfect setting for dried flowers, and an old wooden plane makes a particularly attractive display. Cut a block of florists' foam and wedge it tightly into the hole. Arrange wired clumps of cluster-flowered sunray first, keeping the outline low. Follow with pink *Leucodendron brunia,* allowing it to break out of the shape and dangle low over the sides.

Now add interest and a dash of colour with a few stems of bottlebrush. Put them in singly and keep them short so that their rich colour lies deep within the arrangement.

Soften the effect with a few clumps of grass interspersed throughout. To finish, add contrasting texture with three or four heads of *Leucodendron plumosum* set deep into the display.

A n attractive wall hanging arrangement puts a redundant towel ring to good use. Begin by slicing a sphere of florists' foam in half and cutting away the centre of one piece so that it fits snugly on top of the ring. Secure the foam with a couple of strips of florists' tape.

Form the outline of the arrangement with 'blue leaf' foliage. Balance the general shape with that of the ring but create a spiky effect. Fill in with three or so long-eared pods, packed tightly into the foam, and several clumps of beige cluster-flowered sunray. Concentrate the latter in the centre of the arrangement.

Finish off with large bold clumps of yellow helichrysum (strawflower or everlasting) to brighten up the arrangement and blend with the rich tones of the brass ring.

To add contrast and depth to the arrangement add clumps of rusty brown oak leaves and whispy leaf skeletons to the rhodanthe. Then attach the pink wheat, arranging it amongst the folds of material.

W ith its soft muted tones and shiny satin ribbons this pretty swag will add a touch of romance to your bedroom. You will need a length of muslin, some satin ribbon and a selection of plants — used here are pink rhodanthe (sunray or Swan River everlasting), pink wheat, oak leaves and leaf skeletons. Begin by wiring the plants into large clumps, leaving long 'tails' of wire.

Cut a strip of muslin about 15cm (6in) wide and 100cm (40in) long. Beginning at one end, gather some of the material into a bunch and secure it by wiring on a bunch of rhodanthe. Repeat the process at regular intervals along the length of the fabric, gathering the muslin into soft folds each time.

Make up several double bows using the method described on page 9 and wire them on to the groups of flowers. Use the bows to conceal any wire still showing. Add a couple of long trailing strands of ribbon for the finishing touch. Drape the swag across the end of your bed or around a large mirror.

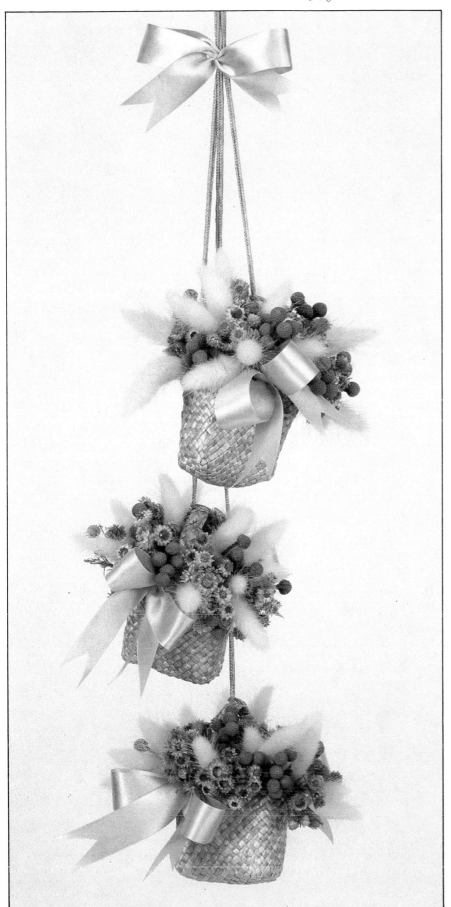

This little collection of hanging baskets would be a pretty addition to a bedroom or bathroom. Take three small straw baskets and place a piece of dry florists' foam inside each one. Take several clumps of wired pink miniature sunray and insert them in the first basket, keeping the flowers close to the foam so that they almost cover it.

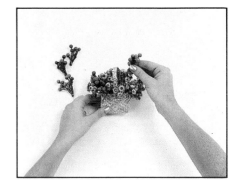

Among the sunray place small pieces of *Leucodendron brunia* to give a contrasting texture. These, along with the sunray, should virtually fill the basket.

Next, bunch together some fluffy heads of rabbit's or hare's tail grass. Keep them taller than the other flowers so that, when slotted in, they rise above the outline.

Finally, make some little bows from pink satin ribbon (following the instructions on page 105) and place one bow on each side of the basket. All three baskets are completed in exactly the same way.

Once the three baskets are finished, tie a piece of co-ordinating cord to each basket handle. Tie all the cords together at the top so that the baskets hang one beneath the other and complete with another pink satin bow.

This fragrant string of pot-pourri bags, designed to hang in the bedroom, makes a delightful gift. First take a square of fabric and, craddling it in the palm of your hand, fill the centre with pot-pourri. Then gather the edges together, turning them in as you do so to make a wide 'hem'. Secure the fabric with wire, making a small ball. Repeat two or more times.

For each bag, make a double bow out of two lengths of wide satin ribbon, tying the second bow round the centre of the first. Gather a few delicate flowers into a small bouquet and wire the stems firmly together. Shown here are deep pink rabbit's or hare's tail grass, some large — and small — flowered helichrysum (strawflower or everlasting) and blue nipplewort (or broom bloom).

These tiny pot-pourri bags are so easy to create, and they make delightful gifts. Take a length of cotton fabric and, using a plate as a pattern, cut out a circle about 25-30cm (10-12in) in diameter. Hem the edge with running stitch, leaving long tails of thread at either end. Cup the fabric circle in your hand as shown and fill it with pot-pourri.

Wire the bunch around the neck of a pot-pourri bag and attach the bow, either with wire or a short length of ribbon. Repeat for the other bags. Finally, take a length of cord and tie the balls together at regular intervals.

Gather the fabric into a tight ball by pulling the threads. Secure with a knot. Wire together a small tight bunch of helichrysum (strawflower or everlasting) using fine silver florists' wire and attach the posy to the bag, threading the wire through the fabric on both sides to secure. (Use a needle to make holes in the fabric first if necessary.)

Make a double bow out of satin ribbon (following the instructions on page 105,) and wire this on to the bag. Finally, cut a length of gold cord about 35cm (15in) long and tie it round the posy, finishing with a double knot. Tie the ends of the cords at the desired length and hang the bag by this loop.

Use some foam spheres, flowers and fabric to make this pretty mobile. Take five spheres of florists' foam. Then cut five circles of fabric, large enough to cover the balls and allowing extra to be gathered up. Experiment with a piece of paper first to determine the correct size of the circle. Wrap each piece of fabric around a ball and secure at the top with silver wire.

Make five small posies from pale blue helichrysum and nipplewort (or broom bloom). Tie the posies with silver wire, leaving a short tail which can then be pushed into the neck of the sphere. Next, cut five lengths of thin cord or ribbon and wind around the top of each ball. Tie a piece of matching ribbon around the neck of the balls and finish with a bow.

These attractive baskets filled with pot-pourri will look very pretty hanging from the dressing table, adding colour and fragrance to your bedroom. Choose a couple of miniature baskets with narrow handles. Head some pink acroclinium (sunray) and glue them round the rim of the baskets. Position them in an uneven ring to make room for the other flowers.

Fill in with heads of larkspur and purple statice, alternating the colours. Glue some of the flower heads half way up the handle on either side.

Wire more of the same flowers into bunches and stick them into a small piece of florists' foam to form a ball of flowers. Tie two pieces of dowling together at the centre with thin cord; leave two long tails of cord for hanging the mobile. Hang four bundles from the arms of the mobile, the fifth from the centre. Attach the floral 'pomander' by a longer cord from the centre.

When the rim is completely covered and the glue dry, make a double bow out of narrow pink ribbon (following the instructions on page 105) and wire it to the top of the handle. Tie a second length of wider, contrasting ribbon around the centre of the bow, leaving long tails for hanging the basket. Finally, fill the basket with pot-pourri.

In this attractive arrangement, peachy coloured flowers set off a small brass trinket box to perfection. Cut a section from a cylinder of florists' foam to fit inside the box and secure with a strip of florists' tape.

Build up the shape of the display with cluster-flowered sunray and a few strands of creamy nipplewort (or broom bloom). The latter will add a fluffy softness to the arrangement.

The perfect Easter present — an attractive egg-shaped gift box filled with a mass of pretty flowers. The flowers have been specially chosen to reflect the colours of the box, creating a very co-ordinated effect. Cut a section from a sphere of florists' foam and put it in the base. Secure it with tape. Place the lid about a third of the way across the foam and again tape in place.

Next add the focal flowers which are peachy South African daisies (a type of helichrysum). Wire them in small groups and intersperse them throughout. Finish off with a few cones to add an interesting contrast of colour and texture.

Build up the outline using brown grass and green amaranthus (love-lies-bleeding). Use some of the amaranthus leaves to add contrast of texture. Intersperse the display with a few small bunches of tiny red helichrysum, placing them well into the arrangement to give depth.

To finish, dot a number of South African daisies (a form of helichrysum) throughout the arrangement. Provided the stems are strong, these can be added singly without wiring.

A delicate posy of dried flowers provides a perfect decoration for any gift. Choose a selection of brightly coloured, small-headed flowers and tie them together with fine wire. The flowers used here are blue larkspur, yellow South African daisy, (a type of helichrysum), small red roses and a touch of golden rod. Wrap a strip of white ribbon around the stems and finish off with a bow.

The posy on this gift box is made up in a similar way, using flowers in a range of colours that match those of the box. The posy contains green amaranthus (love-lies-bleeding), mauve xeranthemums, pink gypsophila (baby's breath), blue larkspur, cream 'cauliflower' and yellow dudinea.

Attach the posies to the gifts with glue. Alternatively you can wire them on. To do this you will need to pierce two small holes in the side of the box. Wrap wire round the stems of the posy and thread it through the holes; secure on the inside.

This pretty miniature display, arranged in a tiny gift box, would make a delightful present. And with all that lavender, it smells as lovely as it looks. First cut a small block of florists' foam and pop it inside the box. Then wire a couple of red ribbons.

Wire together bunches of lavender and pack them into the foam, keeping the arrangement tallest in the middle and splaying it out at the sides. Now scatter tiny, daisy-like glixia or grass daisies throughout; push some deep into the display. Finish off by attaching the two red bows, one to the box, the other higher up on a stem of lavender.

A scallop shell makes an ideal setting for this pretty miniature arrangement. Cut a small block of florists' foam and place it in the bottom of one of the shell halves, securing it with florists' fixative or glue. Position a second shell on top and glue the two shells firmly together as shown.

Wire small clumps of pink gypsophila (baby's breath) and red nipplewort (or broom bloom). Pack them into the florists' foam, forming the outline of the arrangement. Allow a few strands of gypsophila to trail over the edge of the shell.

Three scallop shells provide the perfect setting for a colourful miniature arrangement. First you must carefully bore a hole in the base of each shell using a braddle. Now fix the shells together with wire, fanning two of them out as shown and using the third as a base. Slice a section off a sphere of florists' foam and cut it to fit the base of the shells. Glue the foam in position.

Add several wired strands of blue-dyed *Leucodendron brunia* to provide a strong contrast in colour, and finish off with two or three pieces of red amaranthus (love-lies-bleeding).

Cut off a number of honesty (silver dollar plant) seedheads and insert them singly into the foam, covering it completely. Next add small wired bunches of tiny red roses, concentrating them in the middle. Follow with clumps of golden quaking grass, positioning them so that they fan out from the centre of the arrangement and form a star-shaped outline.

Fill in amongst the quaking grass with clumps of bright yellow cluster-flowered helichrysum (strawflower or everlasting), packing them tightly into the arrangement.

O nce again scallops have been used as the setting for a display, this time in conjunction with a 'fan' of coral to follow through the marine theme. Carefully bore a hole in the base of each shell using a braddle and fix the shells together in an open position with wire. Tape a block of florists' foam into the base and begin to build up the fan with pieces of rust coloured coral.

T he colours of this small conch have been cleverly picked out in the soft pinks and creams of the delicate arrangement. First cut a small block of florists' foam and wedge it into the neck of the shell. Then wire up a few seedheads of honesty (silver dollar plant) and position them in the foam.

Next insert several large heads of soft pink helichrysum (strawflower or everlasting). Fill in any gaps with bunches of small white helichrysum.

Now fill in using wired clumps of cluster-flowered sunray and cream anaphalis, keeping them much shorter than the coral and covering most of the foam. Allow fluffy strands of sunray to spill over the rim of the base shell.

Finally, wire together small bunches of pink rabbit's or hare's tails grass and intersperse them among the arrangement so that they stand up above the other flowers, softly breaking through the outline.

Insert two or three long-eared pods deep into the arrangement to add depth and interest. Finally add the focal flowers by positioning tight groups of South African daisies (a form of helichrysum). Peachy coloured ones have been chosen here to blend with the soft tones of the coral.

These miniature arrangements make pretty novelties to hang on the Christmas tree. One of them is made with cinnamon sticks. Take about three sticks and bind them together with wire. Wire on a double bow made out of gold gift wrap ribbon (following the instructions on page 105) and then add a posy of cones and small red helichrysum (strawflower or everlasting).

To make the other arrangement, first spray a small basket and some walnuts with gold paint. When these are dry, fill the basket with a block of florists' foam. Pack the foam with gold coloured South African daisies (a type of helichrysum) to form a spherical shape.

Push a length of wire through one end of each of the walnuts. Insert three or four nuts into the display, pushing them deep down amongst the flowers. Wire a small bow and attach it to the handle. Finally, hang each arrangement by means of a loop of gold cord.

Here are two more colourful decorations to hang on the Christmas tree. For the red ball, take a length of cord and wire the ends together, forming a loop. Push the wire right the way through a sphere of florists' foam and double it back on itself — into the foam — to secure. Now cover the foam with flowers.

Pack the flowers tightly into the foam to maintain the spherical shape. Those used here are deep red helichrysum (strawflower or everlasting). Fill in with little clumps of red nipplewort (or broom bloom). To finish, gather up and wire small pieces of silver netting, then insert them amongst the flowers.

For this design wire together a few flowers, such as these small white helichrysum and blue-dyed *Leucodendron brunia,* and attach three decorative bells. Gather up a piece of red netting and bind it on to the flowers. Make a double red bow as described on page 105, tie a long piece of ribbon round the middle (by which to hang the decoration) and attach the bow to the netting.

To make this splendid Christmas centrepiece, take a flat circular base such as a cake board and glue a cone of florists' foam to the centre. Then glue or staple a length of gold netting round the edge of the base, gathering it into bunches as you go. Crumple lengths of red fabric or ribbon into double loops and wire the ends. Arrange them in a ring on top of the gold.

Spray a number of Chinese lanterns and lotus seedheads with gold paint. When they are dry, wire the ends and insert them evenly spaced into the cone. Intersperse several long-eared pods throughout, pushing them deep into the arrangement. Add highlights with a few honesty seedheads (silver dollar plant). Then wire together bunches of small red helichrysum (strawflower or everlasting) and dot them among the other plants, adding colour throughout. Finish off by inserting a few groups of white leaf skeletons — about two to three leaves per group.

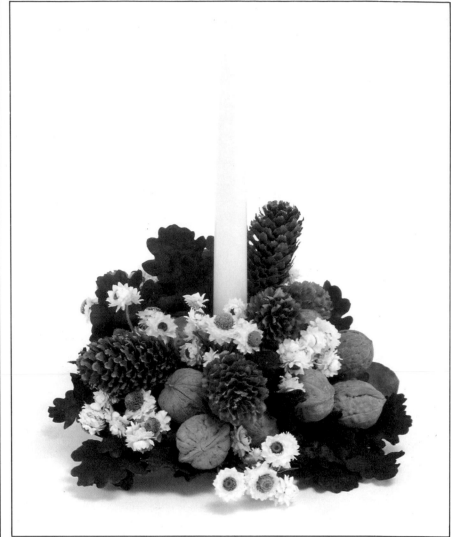

Add style to the dinner table this Christmas with a striking centrepiece. Take a flat circular base — a cork mat or cake base will do — and glue single ruscus leaves around the edge. Stick three blocks of florists' foam on top, keep one taller than the others. Now insert the red candles into the foam, cutting them down as necessary to vary their heights.

Build up the arrangement using gold-sprayed poppy heads, white helichrysum (strawflower or everlasting) and more ruscus leaves. The white adds essential highlights to the arrangement. Finish off by scattering single red roses throughout the display. The colours chosen here are especially for Christmas, but for other times of the year you can choose different colours.

This attractive 'woodland' design makes the perfect centrepiece for a stripped pine table. Begin by making a base out of three large dried leaves, such as these cobra leaves. Glue the leaves together, then glue a block of florists' foam on top. Wire up several cones and walnuts, forcing the wire through the base of the nuts as far as it will go.

Wire together clumps of oak leaves and build up the outline of the display. Now insert the nuts and cones, placing the former in small groups. Keep the shape irregular to make it more interesting. Brighten the display by scattering small clumps of ammobium (sandflower or winged everlasting) throughout. To finish, trim a candle to the required length and push it into the foam.

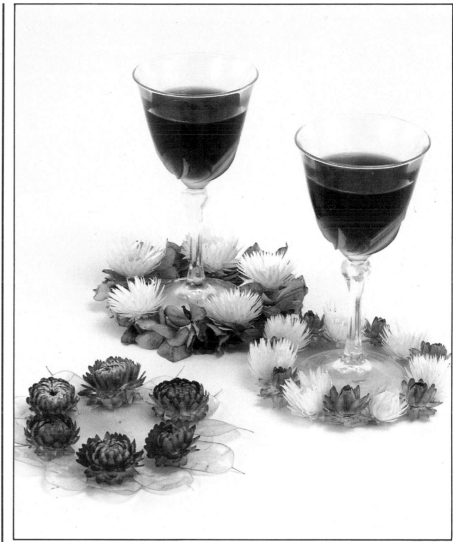

A pair of candlestick holders is transformed by a tightly-packed arrangement of dried flowers. For each stick, cut a sphere of florist's foam in half and hollow out the centre of each piece so that the foam sits snugly round the stem. Wrap a piece of florists' tape around the two halves to hold them together.

Push short stems of orange South African daisy (a form of helichrysum) into the foam, keeping the arrangement spherical. Then fill in with small wired clumps of red helichrysum (strawflower or everlasting) and pink miniature sunray, being sure not to leave any gaps.

Create some pretty coasters using a few flowers and some mother-of-pearl discs. The latter can be bought from any shop specializing in shells. They should measure at least 4cm (1½in) more than the diameter of your glass base. Choose any combination of flowers or seedheads — shown above are helichrysum, honesty and hydrangea. Cut the heads off the plants.

Now create a ring around the edge of a shell by gluing the heads in position. The honesty (silver dollar plant) can be stuck down first — the heads slightly overlapping — and the red helichrysum can be glued down on top at regular intervals. If you are only using helichrysum, alternate the colours for a more interesting effect.

Try decorating some wooden napkin rings with a few dried flowers. You can either cover the ring entirely or make a pretty posy to tie on top. To do the former, simply cover the ring in glue. Then stick masses of tiny flowers on to it until the whole surface is covered. The flowers used here are yellow helichrysum, beige cluster-flowered sunray and poppy seedheads.

To make the posy gather a small square of pink spotted netting in the middle with a long piece of silver wire. Using the same wire, secure strands of beard grass on to the back of the netting, on either side as shown. Next add two pieces of coral, wiring them on in the same way. Finish off by arranging some South African daisies (helichrysum) and cluster-flowered sunray to the front.

Use plenty of fluffy cluster-flowered sunray to hide the wire. Finish off by tying the posy on to the ring with a length of white cord. In this way, by simply untying the cord, each of your supper guests can take home a small memento.

Dried flowers always enhance the dining table, especially when they are used so prettily to decorate the napkins. Buy a length of satin ribbon, choosing a colour to match (or, if you prefer, contrast) that of your napkins. Wire together a small bunch of flowers with silver wire; this posy contains bleached white nipplewort, a couple of long-eared pods and a single red rose.

Take about 35cm (14in) of ribbon per napkin and cut a V-shape in each end. Wrap ribbon round the stalk of the posy and tie a knot at the back, leaving one end longer than the other. Form a loop with the long end (for the napkin to go through) and tie a second knot. Bring the ends to the front of the posy and form a bow. The arrangement can now be put on the napkin.

A ball of colourful flowers adds a welcome splash of colour to an old wooden lamp stand. Begin by slicing a sphere of florists' foam in half and cutting away the centre of each half so that the pieces fit snugly around the stand. Tape the two halves in position as shown.

Wire the flowers into small bunches; used here are blue larkspur, small yellow helichrysum (strawflower or everlasting), green amaranthus (love-lies-bleeding) and dudinea. Insert the plants into the foam, keeping the shape spherical. Position the more spiky larkspur and amaranthus first, then fill in with the dudinea and helichrysum.

A striking and imaginative display transforms a plain lampshade. Begin by wiring together three bunches of flowers, carefully selecting plants that blend well with the colour of your shade. The plants shown here are helichrysum (strawflower or everlasting), cluster-flowered sunray and rat's tail statice.

Make three small holes at the base of the shade. Attach the bunches on to the shade by threading the wires through the holes and securing them at the back. Position the middle bunch upright and the ones on either side running parallel with the rim. Make sure the ends are packed closely together so that none of the stems or wires is showing.

Make your own ear-rings out of dried flowers and mother-of-pearl. The fittings can be bought in a craft shop or good department store, the mother-of-pearl from any shop specializing in shells. For each ear-ring, take two shell discs and pierce a hole through the top of each using a needle. Now thread the ear-ring pin through the holes, and bend it into a loop.

Using silver wire, bind together a small bunch of pink-dyed gypsophila (baby's breath) and a couple of honesty seedheads (silver dollar plant). Make a small pink bow out of satin ribbon and wire it round the posy.

Glue the bunch on to the shells with an all-purpose adhesive. Alternatively, you can make a small hole at the bottom of the disc and wire the posy in position. Finally, attach the discs on to the ear-ring fitting using the looped pin.

Why not decorate your hair on a sunny day with this pretty hair slide? To begin, wire the plants individually; shown here are small pink helichrysum (strawflower or everlasting), South African daisies (also helichrysum), moon grass, leaf skeletons and small cones. Then tie them into a bunch by gradually binding them together with a single piece of silver wire.

To finish simply glue the bunch on to a plastic hair slide using an all-purpose adhesive.

A small straw hat, decorated with a garland of dried flowers, makes a pretty design to hang on the bedroom wall. This particular hat is a small doll's hat. Begin by making three bows out of satin ribbon, as described on page 105. Tie a second length of ribbon round the middle of one of the bows to form the long 'tails' at the back of the hat.

Make a garland to wrap around the crown as follows. Attach some fine florists' wire to a length of string, about 20-25cm (8-10in) from one end. Place a small bunch of flowers over the join and secure with the wire. Add another bunch to cover the stems of the first and bind as before. Continue adding to the garland in this way until it is the desired length.

The flowers used in this garland are red amaranthus (love-lies-bleeding), South African daisy (helichrysum) and golden dryandra. Wrap the garland round the crown and tie the ends of the string together to secure. Wire a couple of bows to the front of the hat and put the other one over the join at the back.

Cut a dash in this stunning and original design made simply from a plain straw hat and just two varieties of flower. First cut a length of pink netting, long enough to wind around the crown of the hat and leave a modest train. Gather the net loosely round the hat and either stitch or wire the fabric to the front and back of the crown.

Using silver wire, tie together a bunch of acroclinium (sunray) and long stems of rat's tail statice. Attach the flowers to the back of the hat, winding the wire securely around the netting. To finish, make a double bow with long trailing tails out of pink satin ribbon following instructions on page 105. Attach the bow to the hat, using it to cover up any wire that still shows.

Even a small courtyard garden can yield a wide range of annuals, perennials, shrubs and trees to provide flowers and foliage to press.

The way nature has fashioned flowers gives us great but short-lived pleasure and delight; capture this delight by pressing flowers and you will have the perfect medium for creating pictures of lasting beauty. To enjoy collecting and pressing you do not have to act like a botanist seeking specimens, but your enjoyment of the countryside will increase as you start to look more closely at what is growing there. Examine the structure of each flower you find and learn to appreciate, for instance, the beauty in a single floret of cow parsley or the exquisite detail in the veining of a rose leaf. Try also to learn the plants' names. You will soon discover which plants are most suitable for pressing and when best to pick them, and to help you, we have illustrated many of the most suitable and colourful ones on page 151.

GATHERING WILD FLOWERS

There is an amazing variety of wild flowers, many of which you may have never previously noticed, and if you gather sparingly from the countryside, you will not harm the plant's future growth. However, do pay attention to the official list of protected and endangered plants that you may not pick. Don't break off stems or pull up roots, but cleanly cut the parts you require with scissors. If you place the cut flowers in an opaque plastic carrier bag, blow it up like a balloon and seal it, they will keep well for a few hours. Don't forget also to gather leaves, tendrils, stems, grasses and seedheads. Among the best leaves are those of carrot, meadowsweet, cow parsley, rose, wild strawberry, silverweed, vetch, cherry, maple, sumach and virginia creeper.

FLOWERS TO GROW OR BUY

Annuals, perennials, shrubs and trees all provide material for pressing and, even if you only have a window box, you can sow alyssum, candytuft, forget-me-knot, lobelia and polyanthus. Succulent and fleshy flowers contain too much moisture to press successfully. Multi-petalled or thick centred flowers such as roses, carnations, chrysanthemums and marguerites do not press satisfactorily as whole flowers but need to be broken into separate parts for pressing.

When picking flowers from the garden, lay them gently in a basket as you cut them, and then dry and press them as soon as possible.

You can still find flowers to press on wet days and in the winter months by visiting a florist where you can purchase a wide range of cut flowers, foliage and pot plants.

WHEN TO PICK AND PRESS

The optimum time to pick flowers is at midday when all the dew has evaporated. Sunny weather is best and rainy days should be avoided. If you have to pick flowers in damp weather, pick whole stems, and stand them indoors in water for a few hours until the flowerheads are dry. Pick flowers at their best, when they have just opened (and before they produce pollen), and gather some buds as well. Look out for varying sizes, unusual shapes, a variety of tints and veining, and interesting visual textures. Remember as you are pressing that you can thin out collective flowerheads such as spiraea, candytuft, wild parsley (Queen Ann's lace) and hydrangea, so do not pass over large headed flowers.

Bought flowers also need immediate attention, so don't be tempted to enjoy their beauty for a few days before pressing, but press them while they are at their best.

Pressed flower arranging need not be an expensive hobby: the design elements (i.e. the flowers) can cost nothing and the equipment is relatively cheap; you can even make your own press at no great expense (see page 150). The amount of money you spend on a design depends largely on the cost of your setting.

Glassine photographic negative bags are ideal for storing your flowers as they are made from acid-free paper which will not attack the plant material. Aids for handling the flowers include a palette knife, tweezers and a paint brush. Miniature flowers like alyssum can be picked up with a needle point and moved about with a fine paint brush. Larger flowers can be picked up with a palette knife or a slightly dampened finger tip and then transferred to the grip of round-nosed tweezers. To fix flowers in a design use latex adhesive. Squeeze a small amount of adhesive on to a palette dish and use a cocktail stick or toothpick to transfer a small dot of it on to the centre back of a flower. Now press the flower in position.

Sprays and larger flowers may need several dots of adhesive to hold them in place, although great care must be taken to ensure that no

adhesive can be seen from the front of the flower as this will ruin the finished look of your design. You should discard the latex as soon as it starts to set in the dish and replace it with a fresh supply.

THE DESIGN BASE

All pictures must be formed on some base; this can be paper, fabric, wood, metal or plastic, and in this book it is referred to as the design base. In choosing textiles, remember that some man-made fabrics are unsuitable in both texture and colour. Old satins and silks are excellent, as are the range of velvets and fine cottons.

Art shops carry a great range of papers and boards. As a design base for pictures, parchment, marbled and watercolour papers are highly suitable. Rough textured watercolour papers and the many shades of heavyweight Ingres paper and twin-wire self-coloured boards are equally suitable for making greeting cards. To make a card, first cut a rectangle of paper or board to the required size, then score (make a crease) along the fold line. To score the card, lay it face down on a cutting board and, using a blunt instrument such as a knitting needle or the blunt edge of a scissor blade, 'rule' firmly down the edge of a ruler. You can now easily fold along this line; if necessary trim the card after it has been folded. Before drawing on the card with a coloured pen it is advisable to mark out your border first in pencil.

Shown below is a range of the equipment you will need for making pressed flower designs. It includes: 1) latex adhesive; 2) cocktail sticks; 3) palette knife; 4) round-nosed tweezers; 5) assorted paint brushes; 6) ruler; 7) pencil; 8) compass; 9) coloured marker pens; 10) varnish; 11) large and small fine scissors; 12) craft knife and, of course, flowers 13).

Large flowers can be picked up on the end of a slightly moistened finger tip before being gripped and moved about with round-nosed tweezers.

After pressing, small flowers can be removed from the tissue by bending the paper round a finger and lifting the flowers off with a paint brush.

Pressed flower designs should always be protected to prevent damage from handling, humidity, exposure to the atmosphere and, as far as possible, from ultraviolet light. Humidity makes pressed flowers curl and exposure to air makes the colours oxidize and quickly fade. To avoid damage from ultraviolet light, which will also bleach colours, all designs should be kept away from direct sunlight, and as glass or acetate will also act as an ultraviolet filter, perhaps the most satisfactory protection is to have the design tightly sealed and covered by a sheet of glass or rigid plastic. As this is not practical in every application, other solutions have been found.

Items used in mounting and framing designs include picture frames, boxes with lids designed to hold craftwork, silks and satin for the design base, ribbons and lace, design papers, acetate sheets, self adhesive 'library' film, a set square, ruler and pencil, and wadding and foam sheets.

SEALING TECHNIQUES

Much of your early work will probably be in the form of greeting cards, and these require a light and flexible covering for the design. Self-adhesive, protective 'library film' is available in rolls with either a gloss or matt finish. It is easy to cut, and after some practice, to smooth over the design. Practise applying library film on a few flower groups of various thickness before you attempt a finished design. Cut a generous piece of film to cover your design, then pull away one edge of the backing paper. Position the film over the design and carefully begin to rub it down with a soft cloth, gradually pulling back the backing paper as you go. The film will need particularly careful rubbing down over thick flowers to avoid trapping air bubbles. When you have finished, trim off any excess film.

Where the greeting card involves an outer card used as a 'mount' for the inner design card, an acetate 'window' can be fixed in position over the aperture (see below), in a way that both enhances the card and protects the pressed flower design beneath.

A slightly heavier and more durable material than library film is 'iron-on' protective film, and again this is available in gloss and matt finishes, and also in a 'linen weave' finish which is ideal for the table mat applications (see page 179). It is a little more expensive than the smooth-on type, and requires some practice (and not too much heat), but it does 'bond' to both flowers and base material very well and the finish gives a professional 'laminated' look.

When decorating objects such as wooden boxes or glass jars, the best way to seal the design is to cover it with several coats of varnish, either matt polyurethane or one of the new ultra hard 'two pack' types, depending on the base material. In these instances, the varnish can also be used to fix the flowers on to the design.

When choosing a picture frame to display pressed flower work, it is most important to make sure that the rebate in the frame (the recess which holds the glass) is deep enough to accept not only the glass, a thin mount, the design paper and the picture back, but also the wadding or foam material that is used to apply pressure to keep the flowers in contact with the glass. The picture back itself must be made of hardboard or plywood, as cardboard will not be strong enough to apply sufficient pressure. The glass must fit accurately into its frame, so that air is, to a great extent, excluded. Recommended wadding material is either synthetic wadding of the sort used in dress making, or the thin plastic foam sheeting used in upholstery. Both are equally suitable, but the depth of the rebate in the frame will decide which is best for each application.

When covering an aperture in a greeting card, apply a line of 'impact' adhesive around the cut-out and, while it is still wet, cover with an acetate sheet.

To cover a design with protective film, gradually pull away the backing paper and rub the film down with a soft cloth, being careful to avoid air bubbles.

Use wadding, as employed in dress making, to pad out frames. It can easily be cut to the correct shape, and a layer pulled off if it is too thick.

To centre the aperture on a mount, draw an 'X' on the reverse of the mount as shown, then draw your aperture with its corners touching the diagonals.

If you have decided that your picture will be enhanced by a mount, it is advisable to prepare this before starting on your design. An artist's watercolour is often set off by a rebated mount, but in a pressed flower picture, unlike a watercolour, you must have the surface of the picture pressed tightly against the glass. If you wish to use a rebated mount, arrange the design on fine fabric which can be pressed through the thickness of the mount by a piece of wadding, cut to fit the aperture (see Victoriana on page 163). If the design material is paper or card, the mount itself should be made of thin paper, and lines can be ruled on it to give an impression of depth.

THE FRAMING SEQUENCE.

The sequence of framing a pressed flower picture depends on the material on which the flowers are being arranged. If it is paper or board, then all the framing work can be done after the picture has been completed, but if it is silk or other woven material, then all the backing material must be in place before work on arranging the flowers is started.

When working with woven material, take the picture back out of the frame and clean it carefully to remove dust and loose particles. Cut a piece of wadding and a piece of your chosen fabric just a little smaller than the back. Lay the back on your work table, centre the wadding on it, and cover with the fabric. If the picture is to have a mount around it, cut the wadding to fit the aperture. When the picture composition is complete, use a dry paint brush to clear away unwanted particles from the base material. Accurately position the mount, carefully lay the cleaned picture glass over it and then lower the frame itself over the glass. Slip your fingers under the picture back, keeping pressure on the frame, turn it over and place it on a soft surface. Now, while still keeping pressure on the back, use a small hammer to gently tack fine panel pins into the frame to hold the back in place. A heavy duty staple gun could be used, but remember that too much vibration at this stage may dislodge some of your carefully arranged flowers. Finally, use picture tape or high-tack masking tape to seal the back and cover the nail heads. Ordinary clear cellulose tape is not suitable as the adhesive dries out, it is not waterproof, and is inclined to shrink. When using rigid, rather than woven, material it is easier to pick up the finished design, lay this on top of the previously prepared wadding and picture back, and then follow the same framing procedures as described above.

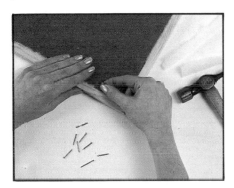

When securing the picture back, keep applying local pressure while you carefully hammer in fine panel pins every 75mm (3in).

When the back is fully secured, use high-tack masking or picture frame tape to seal the gap. This excludes the air and covers the nail heads.

Once pressed, the form of a flower loses its third dimension. So when planning a design, rather than following the guidelines of three-dimensional flower arranging, you should try to create a two-dimensional representation as in a painting.

Look at the designs on the following pages and study the colour, shape and texture of each one. Then look further into the proportions, balance and rhythm of each design. Learn from the harmonizing shades and hues of Falling Leaves on page 157, the contrast of shape, colour and texture of Lazy Daisy on page 154, the mood of cool simplicity of Eastern Inspiration on page 169, the perfect symmetry of Victorian Posy on page 161 and the delicate miniature work of Crystal Miniature on page 175 and the brooch and pendants on page 188. And when you have copied some of these designs, maybe you will be ready to let your personal creativity take over and become an innovator of fresh ideas.

When creating your own designs, spend time choosing your flowers and foliage, carefully considering the colour and shape of each item. Consider also the size and shape of your mount or frame, and decide what shape your design is to take — the line drawings below, illustrating some basic shapes and their focal points, can be used as guidelines. Try to be confident and fix each flower straight down on to the design base rather than move it about from one place to another first — overhandling the flowers will damage their delicate structure.

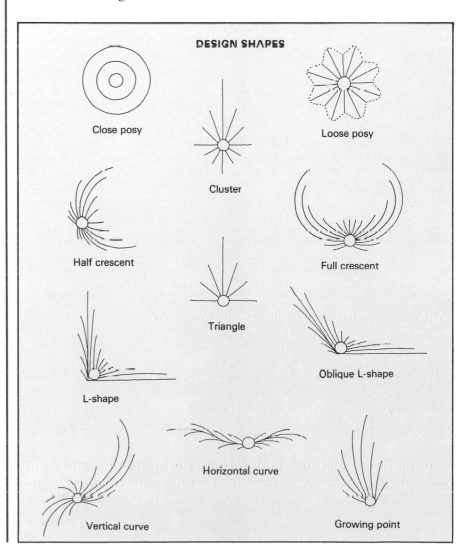

DESIGN SHAPES

Close posy

Loose posy

Cluster

Half crescent

Full crescent

Triangle

Oblique L-shape

L-shape

Horizontal curve

Vertical curve

Growing point

To make your own press, cut two pieces of 10mm (3/8in) plywood measuring 275mm (10¾in) square. Clamp them together and drill 5mm (3/16in) holes in each corner, 18mm (¾in) from the sides. Open up the holes in the top square to 8mm (5/16in). Sand all surfaces, rounding the corners, and apply two coats of matt varnish.

Purchase some 7mm by 200mm (¼in by 8in) fully threaded bolts, with washers and wing-nuts (if not available you can use shorter bolts, 150mm (6in) long). The holes drilled in the bottom square are slightly undersize, but the bolts can be screwed in; add a little 'super' strong glue to the bottom threads just before screwing the bolts home, to fix them permanently.

Take some old newspapers and some thin, double-walled corrugated cardboard and cut them into rectangles 225mm by 255mm (9in by 10in). Cut sheets of blotting paper to the same size then assemble the press by sandwiching layers of blotting paper and newspaper between the cardboard. Each cardboard 'sandwich' should contain 12 sheets of newspaper with two sheets of blotting paper in the centre.

Small flowers and leaves should be placed face down on smooth toilet tissue on top of the blotting paper. Cover them with more tissue before covering with another sheet of blotting paper. Pick sprays of small flowers and press a few whole, but snip off the individual heads of the majority and arrange in rows on the toilet tissue as shown, using a paint brush to move them into position.

Larger flowers such as narcissus 'Sol d'Or' can be placed directly on to the blotting paper, having cut away all the harder parts with sharp scissors. Flowers pressed in profile need to be cut in half lengthways. Put a tab sticking out from between the layers in the press to identify what flowers you have in that layer or layers, and the date when they were put in.

Multi-petalled flowers such as roses and carnations must be broken down into separate petals before pressing and, depending on their size, should be pressed directly between either blotting paper or toilet tissue. The stems, sepals and bracts should be pressed separately in a press devoted to thick items. Use twice as much newspaper as usual between the layers in this press.

Not all leaves are suitable for pressing (see page 146), and of those that are, usually only the younger ones are used. An exception is autumn coloured leaves which often have part of their water content already removed naturally, due to the season. As with flowers, cut or pull the leaves from the stems and arrange neatly on the paper. If they are thick, put them in a press reserved for such material.

Remove all unwanted material from the blossom of trees and shrubs before pressing the flowers. Cut the backs off trumpet shaped flowers when pressing flat, but leave the bloom whole when it is being pressed in profile. When you have finished preparing the press, put the lid on and tighten down gently. At first, tighten the press daily, then less frequently until, between six and eight weeks, the plants are dry.

This beautiful design displays some of the most suitable and certainly the most colourful flowers used for pressing.

1) Russian (silver lace) vine 2) Fools' parsley 3) Spring flowering spiraea 4) Guelder rose (cranberry bush) 5) Whitebeam blossom 6) Blackthorn blossom
7) Meadowsweet 8) Potentilla 9) Narcissus Sol d'Or 10) Golden rod
11) Feverfew 12) Lady's mantle 13) Rose bay willow herb 14) Alyssum 15) Lobelia
16) Lady's bedstraw 17) Primrose 18) Pansy 19) Larkspur 20) Candytuft
21) Hydrangea 22) Cowslip 23) Buttercup 24) Carrot leaves 25) Melilot

26) Creeping cinquefoil 27) Kerria 28) Montbretia 29) Hop trefoil 30) Horsehoe vetch 31) Gypsophila (baby's breath) 32) Speedwell 33) Forget-me-not
34) Flowering currant 35) Japanese crab apple 36) Daisy 37) Heather
38) Delphinium 39) Verbena 40) Love-in-a-mist 41) Snowdrop 42) Rock rose
43) Bent grass 44) Borage 45) Cow parsley 46) Cornflower 47) Spiraea 48) Apple blossom 49) Creeping bent grass 50) Chervil 51) Fuchsia 52) Smoke bush (smoketree).

This card will bring your Valentine a heart 'full of flowers'. Cut a rectangle of pale blue cardboard 400mm by 200mm (16in by 8in); crease and fold it in half. With a craft knife and ruler, cut out a 128mm (5in) square from the centre of the front page. Cut four pieces of lace to fit the sides of this cut-out, mitre the corners and glue in position. Fix a square of acetate to the inside of the 'window'.

Also cut, crease and fold a white card to the above size. On the front page lightly mark out a 'heart' in pencil, to fit within the 'window', adding a few lines to break into the heart. Take a spray of *Acaena* 'Blue Haze' foliage and fix to the right hand top of the heart. Add more leaves and tendrils at various points around the shape, using only pinpoint size dots of adhesive to secure each one to the card.

Apply a tiny dot of adhesive to the top right of the heart and, using the tip of a dry, fine paint brush, tease an alyssum flower over it. Continue to fix tiny flowers all around the heart shape, finishing at the top with a forget-me-not. When the design is complete, carefully glue around the outside edge of the design card, and fix it centrally inside the blue card. Do not glue the back page down.

White satin, flowers and the impression of a church steeple conveys all. Cut a piece of watercolour paper 185mm by 290mm (7¾in by 11½in); crease and fold it in half lengthways. Cut a triangle [base: 115mm (4½in), height: 145mm (6½in)] from the front of the card, then cut a single sheet of paper to fit inside the card; pencil the triangle shape on to it.

Cut 300mm (12in) of 16mm (⅝in) white satin ribbon, fold it and stick it to the apex of the triangle, leaving a loop at the top. Trim the tails to length. Cut a further 600mm (24in) and a 100mm (4in) length of ribbon. Tie a bow in the long one and form bow-like loops in the short one. Sew together and glue to the top of the triangle. Fold the ribbon ends under the card and secure.

Take the single sheet of paper and fix rose leaves and small potentillas inside the tops of the triangle. Gradually add further potentillas, gypsophila and leaves, moving down and outwards to fill the triangle. The finished look is light and spacey, giving a wedding bouquet effect. Glue a piece of acetate over the design and stick the whole sheet to the inside of the folded card.

A garland of pink alyssum and blue forget-me-nots makes a delightful welcome card for a new baby. Cut and fold a blue (or pink) and a white piece of paper to form two cards 150mm (6in) square. Draw and cut out a 95mm (3½in) circle from the centre front of the coloured card. From this circle cut out the crib and edge it as shown with lace, sticking the lace down with glue.

Put the white card inside the coloured card, trim off any surplus paper and trace a feint pencil line through the circle on to the white card. Put the coloured card to one side. Glue the crib on to the centre of the white circle, then form a garland just inside the pencil line using silver southernwood leaves. Next place a cluster of pink alyssum at the quarter points.

Scatter a few forget-me-nots to gently break up the edge of the clusters. Cut a 110mm (4½in) square of white tulle and fix it using latex adhesive on to the inside front cover of the coloured card to cover the hole. Finally, apply glue sparingly all around the inside edge of the front cover and carefully stick the white card in position with the design showing through the window.

Simple daisies can make a chic greeting card. Cut some pale oyster tinted cardboard to 65mm by 165mm (2½in by 6½in). Group three daisies slightly off centre, place another one a little below and to the right and a final one to the left and above the group. Fill in with leaves and stems of hedge bedstraw. Form the focal point with florets of fools' parsley positioned on the most prominent daisy.

This buttercup card brings a ray of sunshine with its greeting. Cut some green paper to 65mm by 165mm (2½in by 6½in). Begin the arrangement with salad burnet and melilot, placing them in the top left corner and bringing them down to form a lazy 'V'. Add buttercups towards the centre, saving the most dominant for the focal point, just off centre, at the base.

Choose purple for the main card, to match the colour with the tips of the daisy petals. Cut the card to 200mm by 215mm (8in by 8½in), score and fold lengthways into a 'tent'. Carefully cover the design with protective film and trim to size. The pale design card against the dark background card will require no border rule. Measure the central position on the background card and glue down the design.

For the best effect, tuck the leaves under the focal buttercup; also ensure that the 'V' is not symmetrical. Cover the design with protective film and trim. Cut a rectangle of cream cardboard 200mm by 215mm (8in by 8½in); crease and fold it lengthways. Draw two rectangles as shown, using a green marker and making the outer rule twice as thick as the inner one. Glue the design inside the border.

Any child would be delighted to receive a pretty flower garden created in real flowers on their birthday card. From green cardboard cut a rectangle 240mm by 175mm (9½in by 7in) in size, crease it and fold it widthways. From an offcut of the green board cut out the required birthday number. Now using white cardboard cut out a rectangle 65mm by 120mm (2½in by 4¾in).

Take a large spray of meadowsweet to make the larger tree and a suitable stem for the trunk. Similarly, make a smaller tree for the other side of the number. Build up the picture by adding verbena, lobelia, cow parsley and daisies to create a colourful border. Cover the design with protective film and carefully trim to size.

Draw a border in pencil on the green card; this will house the design (the border shown is an Edwardian 'reversed corner'). When satisfied with the border, go over it with a dark green fine marker pen. Fix the design within this border.

This traditional Christmas card is easily made. Cut a rectangle of white cardboard to measure 165mm by 65mm (6½in by 2½in). Select a piece of bracken fern about 140mm (5½in) in length. Fix the bracken to the card with spots of glue. Leave sufficient space at the base of this 'tree' for the 'flower pot'. For the star, colour a floret of fools' parsley gold, and glue to the top of the tree.

From red metallic board cut a rectangle 215mm by 200mm (8½in by 8in); crease, and fold in half lengthways. Now draw a rectangle — larger than the white card — on the red card using a gold marker. Cut out a 'flower pot' from some red board, draw on some decorative lines and fix the pot to the tree. Cover the design card with protective film and fix it centrally within the gold border.

Capture the art of bygone days with this card, which can be easily converted into a calendar. From a sheet of acetate, cut an oval 180mm by 250mm (7in by 9¾in). Take one metre (about 40in) of 55mm (2½in) wide gathered cream lace, and using an 'impact' adhesive, glue the gathered edge twice around the acetate oval, about 35mm (1³/₈in) from the edge, to make a double thickness of lace.

Crease and fold in half some heavyweight dark brown cardboard. Mark out an oval on this, the same size as the acetate, but overlapping the folded edge so that, having cut the card out, the two sheets of board are joined for 90mm (3½in) at the fold. Using sprays of Russian (silver lace) vine and leaves of cutleaf Japanese maple *Acer palmatum dissectum,* create a crescent outline on the front.

Fill in the centre and the right arm of the crescent with flowers of feverfew and peach and rust coloured potentillas, and the left arm with buds and flowers of white potentilla. Now use buds and flowers of blackthorn to break up the solidness of the larger flowers. Add interest and colour to the centre with a rock geranium and a leaf of purpleleaf Japanese maple, *Acer palmatum atropurpurea.*

Glue around the outside edge of the front page of the brown card, and fix the acetate sheet and lace centrally over it. Leave this under pressure to dry. Finally, make a small bow from 6mm (¼in) cream satin lace and fix it to the top centre. To convert to a calendar, buy a small calendar block, cover it with brown card and trim with satin ribbon. Suspend this from the main card, then glue the card together.

CAMEO

FALLING LEAVES

The clever harmony of paper, shape and flowers gives this card a three-dimensional effect. Cut a rectangle of maroon coloured cardboard 230mm by 165mm (9in by 6½in) crease it and fold it in half widthways. Place a compass point 65mm (2½in) from the top of the card and in the centre; now draw a circle of 75mm (3in) in diameter and cut this out carefully.

Cut and fold a sheet of grey paper (preferably imitation parchment) to fit inside the maroon card. Using a silver/mauve outline pen in the compass, describe a 56mm (2¼in) circle centrally, and 65mm (2½in) from the top of the paper, so that it will sit within the cut-out in the maroon card. Select a red potentilla, copper carpet foliage and several florets of the hebe 'Midsummer Beauty'.

On the grey paper place a spray of foliage from the centre to the top of the circle. Add more foliage at the right edge and base. Now tuck in some hebe. A potentilla at the base of the circle will form the focal point. Cut a 100mm (4in) square of acetate and fix this inside the maroon card to cover the cut-out. Glue the grey paper inside the card, to the front page, so the design is central in the aperture.

This striking design is ideal for the non flowery. Cut a rectangle from brown cardboard 207mm by 510mm (8¼in by 20in); crease and fold it widthways. Make a similar card from cream cardboard. Cut an aperture in the brown card 140mm by 190mm (5½in by 7½in). Now cut an acetate sheet to 195mm by 240mm (7¾in by 9½in) and fix it inside the brown card over the aperture.

For the design card, cut a single sheet of light brown cardboard to 190mm by 230mm (7½in by 9in). Take a selection of autumn-coloured sumach leaves and, fixing with latex adhesive, make a crab-like shape. Use leaves with curling tips to give movement to the design.

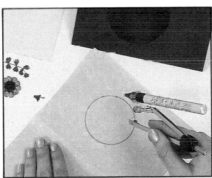

For the centre of the design, use the reverse side of an astrantia flower to show off its beautiful veining. Fix this firmly with adhesive and finally add a floret of fennel over its stalk end. Glue this design centrally to the acetate inside the aperture and when dry, glue the cream card inside the darker brown one by its front page only. Trim off any excess cream card.

Turn offcuts of cardboard into pretty gift tags. Cut a piece each of red metallic and glossy white cardboard 75mm by 100mm (3in by 4in) and fold widthways. Secure a tip of polypody fern to the front of the red card. Spray with gold paint. When dry, lift off the fern, leaving a silhouette. Fix the gold fern to the front of the white card. Punch holes in the top left corners and thread with ribbon.

Cut a piece of single-sided glossy green cardboard 75mm by 100mm (3in by 4in). Crease and fold 40mm (1½in) from the left edge to give a folded card size of 75mm by 60mm (3in by 2½in). With a green marker pen, draw a border inside the larger page. Fix a spray of miniature rose leaves in one corner then form a loose line of guelder rose (cranberry bush) flowers up the page.

Having looked at the construction of an envelope, make a miniature version from a 140mm (5½in) square of paper. Glue the envelope together and line the side flaps with a silver marker. Take wispy foliage, gypsophila (baby's breath) and mauve lobelia and secure them inside the envelope so that they appear to be bursting out. Attach some curled mauve ribbon to the top of the tag.

Take some red and green single-sided cardboard and cut out some sock shapes. Using gold or silver aerosol paint, spray heads of fools' parsley; when dry, secure the best shaped florets to the heels and toes of the socks. Draw a ribbed border at the top of each sock, punch a small hole in the corner, and add coloured ties.

Crease and fold a small piece of yellow cardboard in half and, with your compass pencil just overlapping the fold, draw a 65mm (2½in) circle. Cut this out, leaving the card hinged together by about 30mm (1¼in) at the top. Draw a 50mm (2in) circle in green marker pen on the front cover and fix three daisies in the middle. Re-fold the card and fix a length of thin green ribbon about the fold.

Blue delphiniums and pink candytuft are combined with mauve satin ribbon to create this most attractive bookmark. Select a piece of grey imitation parchment paper and cut a rectangle 200mm by 80mm (8in by 3¼in). Crease and fold it in half lengthways. Open up the folded parchment and on the right hand page fix a loop of 25mm (1in) wide pale mauve ribbon, using latex adhesive. Cut two pieces of ribbon 90mm (3½in) long and trim in a V-shape. Fix these to the foot of the card as shown. Turn the card over to form the design on the page opposite that bearing the ribbons.

The mass of gypsophila (baby's breath) floating up from the bed of pink alyssum gives the impression of thistledown on the breeze. This simple design makes an attractive marker for any book. Cut a strip of black cardboard 300mm by 50mm (12in by 2in). Crease a line 75mm (3in) from the top and fold under. This forms a flap to tuck over a page. Starting about 6mm (¼in) from the base, fix clusters of pink alyssum to a depth of 25mm (1in). Fill in this area with leaves of thyme. From the base build up the gypsophila, starting with the larger flower heads, and retaining some of the stems.

Begin with silverweed leaves facing alternately up the page. Next fix a blue delphinium near the base and overlap with mauve candytuft. Tuck in single candytuft florets under the leaves, gradually decreasing their size up the page and finishing with a few buds. Glue the two pages of card together. Cover both sides with matt protective film (cut to the height of the bookmark and twice the width).

Continue up the bookmark with the gypsophila, gradually increasing the space between the flowers. Stop just under the crease line. Now add smaller gypsophila, taking care not to fill in too much, or the airy effect will be lost. Cut a piece of protective film larger than the book mark, and carefully rub down from the base making sure not to trap any air bubbles. Trim the film flush.

This design is reminiscent of early recorded flower patterns carved in Roman friezes. Choose a landscape-shaped frame about 350mm (14in) wide. Lay the picture back on a bench and cover it with thin wadding. Cut a piece of cream silk to fit the frame, and place on top. Make a soft diamond shape in carrot leaves and add small sprays of lady's mantle, using them to break up the hard outline.

Use green hydrangea florets around the outline and intersperse with small peach coloured potentillas, bringing them in towards the centre. Use larger potentillas further into the centre, tucking in extra foliage to give depth.

Pink potentillas, highlighted against dark foliage and framed in an old gold frame, conjure up thoughts of a Victorian rose garden. Small, old frames can be found in bric-a-brac shops, and are easy to repair and paint. Cut a cream coloured rough surfaced parchment paper to fit the frame, and secure an irregular oval of red-tinged meadowsweet leaves. Place the largest pink potentilla centrally.

Now tuck in large heads of cream candytuft to create lightness. Finally, scatter green florets of guelder rose (cranberry bush) to relieve any solidness. Place the glass and frame over the design/wadding/back 'sandwich'. Slip your fingers underneath with your thumbs on top of the frame. Applying pressure to the sandwich, carefully turn the whole thing over and secure the back.

Fix a further six or seven mixed size potentillas with the largest at the top, interspersing them amongst the foliage to give visual depth. Make the central flower prominent by adding a few leaves under the petals. Finish by adding florets of cow parsnip to create highlights. Place the cleaned glass over the design, turn it over and put it into the frame. Put in some wadding and secure the picture back.

This type of compact posy has retained its popularity for the past century and would fit into any Victorian setting. Cut a piece of imitation parchment paper to fit a circular frame, and lightly pencil on it a 140mm (5½in) diameter circle. Fix tips of carrot leaves around and overlapping the circle. Now add spiraea buds and hedge parsley florets to fill out the circle.

Next take light peach coloured rose petals and fix them around and over the base of the leaves. Turn the paper in an anti-clockwise direction as each petal is secured, overlapping its neighbour, to ensure that you keep a good shape. Now secure a second row of petals over the first.

Take some variegated dogwood leaves and secure them in a circle, positioning the tips half way from the top of the second row of petals. Keep moving the card round in an anti-clockwise direction as you fix the leaves. Now fix a circle of pale blue lobelia over the dogwood.

Fix a circle of open spiraea flowers between the first and second row of rose petals, and forget-me-not and hedge parsley florets below the second row of petals. Finally, fix a ring of small rose petals within the lobelia circle and secure a cream potentilla in the centre. Cut a circular mount to fit the frame, allowing space at the perimeter of the design. Frame as usual.

The white and blue flowers against a dark background suggests the dawning of a new day. Select a round frame and cut a circle of blue-green paper to fit inside. Secure variegated dogwood leaves in a full crescent, with larger leaves towards the base of the crescent and smaller ones at the tips.

Place a large delphinium at the centre of the crescent. Now use lady's mantle sprays and white melilot spikes to break up the outline. Buds of feverfew and small white potentillas are added towards the ends of the crescent.

Capture the beauty of that special rose. This design needs a round frame about 150mm (6in) in diameter. Cut a mount from coloured paper, then cut a white card to fit the frame. Lay the mount over the white card and very lightly pencil in the inside diameter of the mount. Take single rose leaves and fix each — slightly overlapping — with the leaf tips about 3mm (1/8in) from the pencilled circle.

Tuck in small buds of delphinium to follow round the shape. Now use large white potentillas and small delphiniums to make an interesting strong centre, and finish the shape with a few further sprays of lady's mantle. Frame in the usual manner with light wadding or plastic foam sheeting under the frame back to provide the necessary pressure to keep the picture in place.

Select large rose petals and repeat the process, with the top of the petals overlapping the leaves by 6mm (1/4in). Both the leaves and petals need to be fixed with very small dabs of latex adhesive. When the glue has dried, carefully rub out the pencil line and blow away the rubbings.

Now form an inner circle with smaller petals in the same way. Select the centre part of a rock rose, put a small dot of adhesive right in the middle of the rose ring, and using a palette knife, slide the rock rose centre in position. Finally, place the mount over the design card, being careful to centre it, and position the cleaned glass over both. Transfer them to the frame and secure the back.

VICTORIAN OVAL

Overtones of lace and a combination of creeping vines and burgundy flowers give a Victorian flavour to this delightful design. Use an oval frame 400mm (16in) across with a burgundy mount, cut slighty wider than your chosen lace. Gather the lace around the mount, folding it at the inside edge and glueing it to the outside edge of the mount.

Cut an oval of 12mm (½in) cellulose wadding to fit exactly the centre of the mount aperture. Place the picture back face up on your bench and put the wadding in the centre. Cover this with oyster coloured silk, trimmed slightly smaller than the frame. Lay autumn leaves to form a crescent and add trails of Russian (silver lace) vine and fuchsia buds to break up the outline.

Add cream potentillas, fools' parsley, buds of cherry blossom and frost-tinged hydrangeas. Create a slightly solid design to give the Victorian look, then lighten the effect with the laced mount, carefully positioning the latter over the design. Next place the cleaned glass over the mount, then finish off the 'sandwich' by adding the picture frame.

Memories of a country walk will float back when you view the mixture of grasses and leaves you have gathered and prettily arranged on a sky blue background, framed in natural wood. Fresh young grass stalks, seedheads and small leaves are most suitable; make a 'growing point' using reed canary grass, rice (cord) grass, cocksfoot (orchard) grass and quaking grass.

Having fixed the grasses down with latex adhesive, cut off the excess stems to leave a clear space in the centre. Now fill this in with more grasses, trimming as you go. Finish at the bottom centre with a few knapweed buds and vetch foliage, to give the impression of a 'growing point'. The design is framed without a mount to give a feeling of space.

This frame, reminiscent of garden furniture, and the colourful design suggest bright summer days sitting in the garden. Select cream and brown marbled paper for the background. Fix bracken fern, polypody fern and salad burnet to make an irregular fan shape, taking care to make it asymmetrical.

Use meadowsweet and yellow melilot sprays to fill in between the foliage. Now, using sprays and buds of montbretia, introduce some colour to the left of the design and put a bold spray in the bottom right corner. Create the focal point with a yellow potentilla flower nestled in amongst a large spray of hedge parsley.

Harmonize the whole arrangement by filling in with single flowers of montbretia. Now add further potentilla flowers using a palette knife to help tuck some of the petals under the hedge parsley spray. Place the cleaned glass over the completed design, turn it over and place face down in the picture frame. Add the wadding and picture back and seal it well.

The new 'two pack' varnish makes it possible to seal flowers to many surfaces without altering their form or colour. Once you have mixed the varnish, you will have about two hours to complete each stage. From an art shop buy a sheet of polystyrene foam sandwiched between two lightweight sheets of drawing board. Cut a piece 230mm by 550mm (9in by 20in) with a ruler and craft knife.

Paint on the board a pale coloured sky and field with water colour paints, and stipple them to achieve a soft effect. Set aside to dry completely.

When the background is dry, mix together a little of the two pack varnish, and apply a coat to the top two thirds of the board. Using a palette knife, start placing various grasses at intervals along the middle section of the board. The varnish will hold them in place. Use a good selection: rye grass, bearded twitch grass, brome grass, meadow fescue and squirrel tailed fescue.

Continue to build up the meadow with crested dog's tail grass, quaking grass, rough meadow grass, tufted hair grass, loose silky bent grass, hare's tail grass and some fennel florets. On the right hand side add yarrow leaves, polypody fern, camomile leaves and spiraea buds to give the impression of distant trees.

Paint a thin line of varnish along the bottom 12mm (½in) and cover this with small dark green leaves to make a solid base. Re-varnish the bottom left half and fill in with more grasses, now adding common knotgrass, knapweed, shepherd's purse, speedwell, periwinkle, daisies, buttercups, lady's bedstraw, wild carrot (Queen Ann's lace), melilot and vetch. Now re-varnish the bottom right half.

Apply these same plants to the bottom right side. Finally, give two thin coats of varnish (allowing the first to be quite dry before applying the second) to the whole picture area. This delightful scene requires no frame, so simply fix a small ring to the back and hang it on the wall for all to admire.

Here's a charming way to provide the bride with an everlasting memento of her wedding day. And there should be plenty of flowers left over to make gifts for other special guests as well, including yourself! See opposite for the bride's picture and on the following pages for guidelines to making the other designs: 153, 161, 162, 169, 173 and 174.

Continue to add more flowers and leaves. If you are using polyanthus, you will find the flowers appear very thin after pressing, so place one on top of another to give greater depth. Using some coloured ribbons saved from the bouquet, stick three short lengths together, and add two loops to form a bow. Fix this in position on one side of the bouquet and add a short length to the other side.

Make up some rosebuds as before and use these to fill in the centre of the design along with some foliage and other flowers; used here are polyanthus, carnation and gypsophila (baby's breath).

If you intend to press the bouquet, ensure the florist does not spray the flowers. Seal the bouquet as soon as possible in a dry plastic box on a bed of tissue paper and keep it in a cool place until you are ready to press it — preferably the next day. Dismantle the bouquet by carefully unwiring each item then press the flowers as described on page 150, leaving under pressure for six weeks.

Make a large open rose by arranging a ring of small overlapping petals on top of a large base petal. Fix sepals to the back of the rose so that they extend beyond the petals and bed the flower in the centre of the design. When complete, frame the picture as usual. The remaining flowers, together with the bridesmaids' bouquets, can be used to make gifts for other members of the wedding party.

Mask a photograph of the bouquet to match the shape of your chosen frame — this will help you to follow the bouquet's design more easily. Lay the picture backing on your work surface and cover it with paper, wadding and ivory silk, cut to size. Using latex adhesive to fix the flowers, copy the shower trail. Make the rosebuds from a few small petals and a couple of sepals.

Now build up the outline with the foliage, moulding the shape to fit comfortably into the frame. Using the photograph as reference, add flowers and buds to the design. Form carnation buds with a few sepals to several petals.

This beautiful ruby satin bow makes a perfect setting for specimen pressings. Take 2½m (2¾yd) of 75mm (3in) wide ribbon, and cut it into three lengths: 500mm (20in), 580mm (23in), and 1.42m (56in). Fold the shortest length, ends to centre, to form a bow and gather the centre using needle and thread. Do the same with the next longest length.

Place the smaller bow on top of the larger one, gather them tightly at the centre, and stitch together. Fold the longest length approximately in half around the centre of the double bow, and sew together at the back to form the knot of the finished bow. Also sew in a small curtain ring at the back by which to hang the design. Trim the ends of the ribbon as shown.

Cut three ovals from beige cartridge paper to fit some miniature plaques. Using a fine pen, write the botanical names of your specimens neatly at the bottom of the ovals. For the first oval, arrange stems, foliage and flowers of forget-me-not to simulate a growing plant. When satisfied with their positioning, fix down with latex adhesive and re-assemble the plaque.

For the second oval, take a large heart's ease (Johnny-jump-up) and fix it one third of the way up from the base, then add further flowers finishing with the smallest at the top. Now introduce heart's ease leaves to give the appearance of a vigorous young plant. When satisfied, fix in position and then carefully assemble within the plaque.

Place a curved stem in the centre of the third oval and fix borage flowers and buds along the stem in a natural way so that it resembles the top of a growing stem. As before, when you have completed the picture, assemble the plaque. Take the three plaques, and arrange them down the ribbon at regular intervals. Now sew them in place, parting the ribbons slightly.

These double peonies should be picked when just open. Strip off the petals and bracts and press between layers of blotting paper, tightening the press daily. After five days change the paper, then tighten the press every three days until ready. Cut some heavy watercolour paper to 520mm by 215mm (20½in by 8½in) and arrange peony leaves in two groups as shown.

Next, fix bamboo leaf sprays, starting at one corner and curving them down towards the opposite corner. Intersperse some sprays between the peony leaf groups.

Away from the picture area, assemble the peony buds. Fix a bract on top of a small petal for the top bud, and another bract on top of two or three petals for the second bud. For the largest bud, use two bracts over four petals. Pick up the buds with tweezers and fix them in position with adhesive, tucking them under the bamboo leaves.

Create the smaller of the two open flowers in position over the ring of peony leaves as follows: using medium sized peony petals, form a ring of overlapping petals around the base of the leaves. Now add a second ring of smaller petals inside the first, and complete the flower by adding wild carrot (Queen Ann's lace) florets to the centre.

Add a few more bamboo leaves to the large ring of peony leaves, and then use some large petals for making the irregular outer circle of the second flower. Fill in with smaller petals to make the second and third circles, and create a centre with wild carrot florets. When complete, make certain that all debris is brushed from the paper before framing the picture.

The clever use of smoke bush (smoketree) on green velvet helps to create a soft misty effect in this striking picture. Remove the back from a rustic frame and cover with wadding and dark green velvet. Start the design by fixing sprays of young ash tree leaves in the shape shown.

Add brown beech leaves and small buds of black knapweed to fill in the outline and create a 'bagpipe' shape.

Suggestions of the 'pipes' are represented by seed heads of pendulous sedge and bottle sedge. Add some spikes of heather to create a solid mass in the centre.

Finally soften the outline by adding the wispy flowers of smoke bush around the edges of the 'bagpipe'. When the design is complete, take care to remove all the dust and pollen from the velvet before placing the cleaned picture glass and frame over it. Slide the frame to the edge of the table and, gripping it firmly, turn it over. Apply pressure to the back of the frame, tack on and seal.

This design's 'just picked' look hides the meticulous care that is needed to make the arrangement. Use cream coloured silk for the background and a good mixture of foliage and grasses for the outline. Secure short stems at the base to represent the flower stalks. Add mixed flowers over the foliage, starting at the top with the palest colours.

Carry on down the sides of the design and then place a head of sweet cicely in the centre to cover the tops of the stems (see above). Start adding the stronger coloured flowers, fixing a large yellow *Kerria* over the sweet cicely. Finally, soften the outline by adding flowers that droop down to the base of the bunch (see below). Choose a rustic frame, pad this out and closely seal the back.

The colours and fine grain of this beautiful cherrywood box are complemented by the subtle arrangement of autumnal foliage. Begin by creating and 'L' shaped outline with leaves of Japanese maple, autumn cherry, willow, wayfaring tree, hawthorn, sumach and smoke bush (smoketree).

Continue adding the foliage, using sufficient adhesive to fix each leaf securely. Trim any overlapping pieces, so as to avoid excess bulkiness. When you are happy with the shape, coat it with a thin layer of matt varnish.

Now add small buds of blue lobelia, creating a sweeping curve throughout the outline. Use larger, open flowers in a cluster at the left and base of the design to form the focal point. Finish with two thin coats of varnish.

These delicate designs transform ordinary thick candles. But be very careful not to let the candle burn down below the protective film, as the designs are not flameproof! For the yellow candle fix three autumn sumach leaves in a spray with latex adhesive. Repeat twice around the candle.

This is a simple but elegant way to use empty gift boxes as containers for pot-pourri. We have selected a green and a black box. Take the lid off one of the boxes and lightly secure three whole flower heads of cow parsley diagonally across it. With aerosol spray paint, give the top of the box two light coats of gold paint.

When the paint is dry, remove the parsley to reveal the unsprayed part of the box. This shows up as a pretty pattern through the paint. Now fix the gold sprayed cow parsley to the other box lid. These boxes are filled with 'Noel' pot-pourri, which is a festive mixture of small cones, tree bark and citrus peel. Cover the pot-pourri with cling film (plastic wrap) before replacing the lids.

The other candle is offset with five pink larkspur flowers fixed around the base. Rue leaves are tucked in and around the flowers. Finally, add some larkspur buds a little above the foliage. Carefully cover the designs on both candles with protective film, allowing an extra 5mm (¼in) above the design. Rub the film down carefully and avoid trapping any air bubbles.

This heart shaped trinket box makes a pretty gift for someone you love. Cut a heart shaped piece of ivory silk to fit the lid. Now cut 75mm (3in) of 6mm (¼in) wide ivory satin ribbon. Fold the ribbon in half, trim each end and glue to a small geranium leaf. Fix this near the point of the heart as shown.

Fix another leaf on top of the fold in the ribbon and then add leaves alternatively to the right and the left, building up a heart shaped outline. When the shape is complete, fix florets of cow parsley over the inner edge of the leaves.

The dramatic effect of white flowers against a black silk background enhances the silver plated trinket box to create a sophisticated gift. These trinket boxes can be readily purchased from craft shops. Open up the lid assembly and take out the foam padding. Cut a circle of black silk to cover the padding.

Secure sprays of miniature variegated rose leaves in a crescent shape. Now add sprays and single flowers of gypsophila (baby's breath), tucking the stems under the leaves where necessary.

Fill the centre of the heart with rich red verbena. Finally, fix a small ivory satin bow to the top of the heart as shown below and assemble the box lid according to the manufacturer's instructions.

Starting at the tips of the crescent, and building to the centre, add buds and flowers of feverfew. Place a large full flower of feverfew towards the bottom centre to create a focal point. When the design is complete, cover it with the plastic sheet from the lid, and assemble according to the manufacturer's instructions.

Once you have gained confidence in using larger flowers, you will find this miniature design an exciting challenge. Buy a miniature crystal bowl (available from good craft shops) and use the white card from its lid as the design card. Start by fixing the tiny foliage of shepherd's purse in place to make a full crescent outline.

Fill in the outline with florets of yellow and pink alyssum and elderberry flowers. To fix the flowers in position first place a tiny spot of latex adhesive in the required place and, using a paint brush, gently tease a flower over it, then press it to secure.

Finally, tuck in heart's ease (Johnny-jump-up), keeping the largest to make a focal point towards the bottom centre of the design. Place the plastic circle from the lid over the finished design, and assemble according to the maker's instructions.

Another pretty design for a trinket box lid. Cut an oval from pale green cardboard to fit the lid. Form a full crescent shape outline with sprays of miniature rose leaves and hairy tare.

Now follow the outline with tendrils and buds of vetch. For the focal point, choose an open peach potentilla and fix it to the base of the crescent, slightly off centre.

With the aid of a palette knife, tuck a green hydrangea floret under the right side of the focal flower. Add a few small guelder roses (cranberry bush flowers) and slip a second potentilla between the foliage. To complete the design tuck another hydrangea floret and a third potentilla into the design just above the focal flower to balance the arrangement. Assemble the lid as instructed.

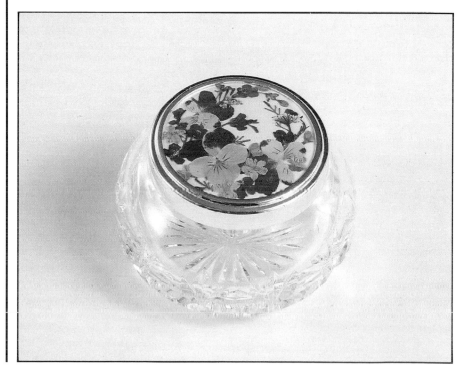

Paperweights, specially designed to hold craftwork, are readily available from craft suppliers. In this design, a stunning arrangement for that special birthday is easily created with a few flowers. Begin by cutting a black card to fit the oval recess of the paperweight. Paint the figure '21' in white to the right of the oval.

Break up mugwort foliage and, keeping the white underside uppermost, fit it to the card following the outline of the oval. Where the foliage meets the '21', add some budded sprays of gypsophila (baby's breath).

Intersperse a few open flowers of gypsophila amongst the foliage then create the focal point with a large open flower of white larkspur. To complete the design, tuck a small larkspur flower under the leaves above the focal point, and place a larkspur bud below. Position the design card inside the recess of the paperweight, pad out with foam if necessary, and seal with the self-adhesive baize.

If you don't feel up to scripting the words for this attractive paperweight design, see if you can locate a caligrapher or illustrator to do it for you. Cut the paper on which the words are inscribed to fit into the paperweight's recess. Surround your quotation or verse with several sprigs of thyme foliage.

Intersperse the foliage with a pretty range of minute flowers: shown here are spiraea, forget-me-not, red alyssum, star of Bethlehem, buds of Japanese crab apple, thyme and melilot. To fix each flower, put a dot of latex adhesive in the required place on the design card and tease the flower into position with a paintbrush; press lightly to secure.

To complete the design add a few buds and flowers of the hebe 'Simon Delux' and some yellow alyssum. Finally, place a heart's ease (Johnny-jump-up) to the right of the verse before fitting the design into the paperweight and sealing it with the self-adhesive baize supplied.

Not every arrangement need be pretty and feminine. This design is perfect for any man's desk. Cut a piece of cardboard to fit the recess of the paperweight and place a thin layer of latex adhesive along one edge. Fix to the strip of adhesive a selection of leaves, overlapping each other and the edge. Repeat for the other three sides then trim the leaves flush with the side of the cardboard.

Fill in the centre of the design with smaller leaves. Shown here are hawthorn, virginia creeper, flowering cherry, spiraea, *Euonymus*, smoke bush (smoketree), and *Acaena* 'Copper Carpet'. Overlap the foliage randomly to create a more natural appearance.

Commemorate a special event with this highly individual paperweight. Cut a circle of white cardboard to fit inside the recess of the paperweight. Divide the circle into eight equal segments using a fine pencil, then draw a 25mm (1in) gold circle in the centre. Outline the circle inside and out with a black pen and mark out the segments with gold.

When the design is complete, fit it into the recess of the paperweight. If necessary, pad out with foam before sealing with the self-adhesive baize supplied.

Inside the centre circle write the date that you wish to commemorate with a black pen. Now form a background on each segment with small sprays of yarrow foliage. Secure them with the stems toward the centre.

On two opposite segments place several buds of pale pink candytuft and an open flower at the centre. In the opposing segments use single flowers of yellow melilot, red alyssum and segments of sweet cicely. Put the design inside the paperweight recess and pad out with foam if necessary. Seal the design with the self-adhesive baize supplied.

Afternoon tea takes on real elegance with this striking tray purchased from craft suppliers. Fix a cluster of autumn plumbago leaves at one end of the oval card (supplied with the tray) and at the other end fix a smaller cluster of plumbago and autumn wild strawberry leaves. Now enlarge and fill out these two clusters with leaf sprays of *Acaena* 'Blue Haze'. Keep each cluster fairly oval in shape.

Working first on the smaller cluster, create a focal point with a red-tinged green hydrangea flower sitting on top of a wild carrot (Queen Ann's lace) flowerhead. Now form a gentle curve of pink potentilla across the top of the cluster and finish off with green hydrangea and red saxifrage. For the focal point of the larger cluster place a deep red potentilla on top of a head of wild carrot.

To add depth, tuck some pink potentilla and red-tinged hydrangea under the carrot head. Now place two smaller 'Red Ace' potentillas above the focal point. Make a gentle diagonal curve into the centre of the design with buds of Japanese crab apple and finish off with sprays of greyhair grass. Reassemble the tray according to the manufacturer's instructions.

An ingenious idea which adds individuality to any table setting. Begin by cutting a rectangle of hardboard 215mm by 280mm (8½in by 11in). Round off the corners with sandpaper. Next, cut a piece of green marbled paper to fit the hardboard. Draw two double-lined borders with green pen in opposite corners, as shown.

Using foliage of the *Ranunculus* 'Bachelor's Buttons', make a triangular shape in the top left corner and an 'L' shape in the bottom right. Add fuchsias to the triangle, beginning with a bud at the apex, gradually adding more open flowers and finishing at the widest part with a full flower. Repeat the process on the 'L' shape, using fuchsia buds at the tips and a full flower in the centre.

Seal the design with a transparent linen-surface covering — the type that is ironed on. Trim the edges. Now cover the back of the design card with latex adhesive and fix carefully on to the hardboard. Finally, fix a rectangle of green felt on to the reverse side of the table mat.

These glass drinks coasters — readily available from craft shops — lend themselves to a carnation display. Cut a circle of moss green paper to fit into the recess of the large bottle coaster. Now fix large petals of yellow carnation, overlapping them slightly, to form an outer circle.

Fill in the outer circle with smaller carnation petals to create a second circle. Small petals from the centre of the carnation make up the final inner circle. To complete the display fix cow parsley florets to the centre.

Fit the design card into the recess of the bottle coaster and seal with the circle of baize supplied. Repeat this process for each drinks coaster, using different colours for an attractive display.

The combination of cream coloured blossom and lace prettily complement traditional china at the dinner table. Cut a rectangle of dark brown cardboard 110mm by 80mm (4½in by 3¼in). Crease and fold it widthways to form a 'tent'. Using a gold marker pen carefully write the desired name in the centre of the top page.

Take about 300mm (12in) of cream lace and, starting about three quarters of the way along the folded edge, fix it to the card with a little latex adhesive. Pinch the lace to form gathers as you round the corners and fix with a little extra adhesive.

Select a colour to complement the bride's attendants and these place cards will enhance the wedding feast. Cut a rectangle of cardboard 170mm by 65mm (6½in by 2½in); crease and fold it widthways. Select some grained silver paper and, using a template, mark and cut out an oval 37mm by 55mm (1½in by 2¼in). Trim the silver paper to 55mm by 75mm (2¼in by 3in), keeping the oval centred.

Glue the silver paper cut-out centrally to the front of the card using a glue pen. With latex adhesive, fix some carrot leaves in a crescent shape at the top right corner, and slightly smaller ones to the bottom left. Place a small head of fools' parsley centrally on each crescent.

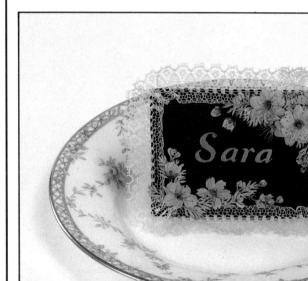

Using the buds and open flowers of blackthorn, make an 'L' shape at the top right corner. Use an open flower to cover the join in the lace. Create the focal point by using a pair of open flowers, glued one on top of the other. This will also give these delicate flowers greater depth. Make a similar shape, but without the focal point, at the bottom left corner.

Build up on these corner designs with pink candytuft florets and more pieces of fools' parsley to give an elegant balance.

This napkin holder offers a delightful alternative to the standard napkin ring. Cut 1½m (5ft) of 40mm (1½in) wide peach satin ribbon. About 100mm (4in) from one end fix a peach potentilla. Tuck melilot foliage above and below this, then add three spikes of white melilot above. Arrange an identical display about 50mm (2in) from the other end of the ribbon.

Cut two strips of protective film, about 200mm (8in) long, and cover the ends of the ribbon. Firmly stroke out any air bubbles. Trim the ends of the ribbon into 'V' shapes. Finally, tie the ribbon into a generous bow around a triangular napkin arrangement, allowing one end to fall slightly longer than the other, as shown.

These simple but attractive napkin rings can be purchased from craft suppliers and make a perfect complement to any dinner party. On a strip of green marbled cardboard, mark out an oval 50mm by 37mm (2in by 1¼in) with a green pen. Inside this oval, mark out a smaller one, also in green. You will need a template to achieve an accurate shape.

Repeat this procedure using a wide range of different coloured flowers; used here are buttercup, blue lobelia, daisy, red verbena and different varieties of pansy.

In the centre of the ovals, fix an attractive flowerhead. Cover the design with protective film, smoothing out any air bubbles. With the aid of a steel rule and craft knife, trim the strip to fit the napkin holder.

SUFFOLK LETTER RACK

COAT RACK

Russian vine (silver lace vine) is a natural creeper, so it is in an ideal setting, creeping and climbing over this pine coat rack. First, sand the wood thoroughly before applying one coat of 'two pack' varnish.

With the aid of a palette knife, start to adhere sprays of Russian vine to the varnish, putting them at various heights along the length of the rack. Add a few leaves and single sprays to fill in.

Cover the vine stem ends as you go with the feathery foliage of camomile. When the design is complete, and the varnish dry, apply two further coats of varnish.

Feverfew flowers and rose leaves transform a simple letter rack into a handsome writing table accessory. Start by coating the front face of the bottom rack with matt varnish. Place a spray of rose leaves on the left hand side, pointing upwards from the bottom corner. Add a feverfew bud just above the first leaf and a flower at the end of the spray.

Position a second rose leaf spray next to the first, this time pointing it downwards. Continue in this way across the rack, adding feverfew flowers between the sprays. When the design is dry, give two further coats of thin varnish. Follow the whole procedure once again for the top rack.

Once again, a plain wooden container is enhanced by the addition of a few flowers. Begin by varnishing the front of the utensil holder. With a palette knife gently ease into position an oval outline of feverfew foliage.

Plain pine book ends can easily be decorated using a selection of pressed flowers. Begin by painting one book end with matt varnish. While the varnish is still sticky, create a loose triangular shape, starting with a miniature rose leaf spray and buds of blue delphinium.

Starting at the top of the outline, fill in with buds of feverfew, gradually working down the design with both buds and flowers. Finish at the base of the foliage with the largest feverfew flowers to create a focal point. Tuck in extra leaves to fill any gaps and when the design is dry, finish with four further coats of varnish.

Working in gentle curves, position peach potentillas to the left and delphiniums to the right of the design. Scatter spiraea 'Snowball' florets throughout, and finish by extending the outline with a few small leaves. When dry, coat the design again with two thin coats of matt varnish.

These specially designed door plates, available from craft suppliers, can be decorated to suit the decor of any room. Cut a piece of protective film to cover the back of the plate and a piece of foam to fit the centre of the plate without overlapping the holes. Then cut a rectangle of coloured cardboard to fit the recess and punch holes in the corners to match those in the plate.

Create the design above with the narcissus 'Sol d'Or' and tiny florets of cornflower. Place the design card in the recess at the back of the plate, pad out with the foam and seal the back with protective film. The design below is made with sprays of montbretia buds, autumn leaves and potentilla. The third example contains specimens of meadowsweet, buttercup and cowslip.

Now return to the top rung. Place three rose leaves in the centre of the garland, and add a small spray of cow parsley and florets of red alyssum to the tip of each leaf.

Position a single larkspur bud at either end of the garland. Now take two medium sized larkspur flowers and place them equidistant from the centre, at the high points of the garland. Finish with a large pink larkspur in the centre. The completed design is shown below on a larger scale to help you see more detail.

When both rungs have dried completely, apply two or three coats of varnish to seal the designs. Be quite sure that each coat is dry before applying the next.

This pretty chalet-style chair is child size, but you can just as easily create the design shown here on a full scale chair. Lay the chair down on to your work surface and coat the front of the top rung with 'two pack' varnish. Now form a wavy garland using the trailing stems of 'mind-your-own-business' plant, leaving a gap in the middle. In between the leaves place single florets of red alyssum.

When dry, apply another thin coat of varnish in preparation for the next flowers. Now varnish the lower rung. Place a large red alyssum in the centre and add a short trail of mind-your-own-business to the left. At the end of this trail add another, smaller head of alyssum, before finishing with just a few mind-your-own-business leaves. This forms half the garland. Repeat on the right side.

Blue lobelia is an attractive addition to plain yellow enamel. Start by marking out a rectangular area on the side of the pot with masking tape. Now lay the pot on its side, securing it to your work surface with an adhesive putty such as Blu-Tack. Paint the area with a thin coat of 'two pack' varnish. Take care the varnish does not build up at the tape edge and form a ridge.

While the first coat of varnish is still sticky, position several carrot leaves to form a teardrop shape outline. When this design is completely dry, add another coat of varnish.

Now, fill in with the flowers. Use lobelia, beginning with buds at the top and coming down to the base with larger flowers. Fill in any gaps with foliage and add a couple of budded stems at the base to create a natural effect. When this is dry, remove the tape and give a final coat of varnish, feathering the edges by wiping them with a lint-free cloth.

This type of white enamel canister can be bought either new or second hand. Secure the canister to your work surface with blobs of adhesive putty. Now take a large head of mauve candytuft and fit to the centre of the canister with latex adhesive. Surround the flower with salad burnet leaves and add two more candytuft flowers on either side. Paint over the design with 'two pack' varnish.

For the canister lid, coat with varnish before positioning a circle of salad burnet leaves — slightly apart — around the knob. Fill in between the leaves with large, single candytuft flowers. When dry, seal this design with two thin coats of varnish, feathering the edges with a lint-free cloth.

Transform a 'sample' coffee jar into a pretty herb or spice container. If you have several of these jars, you can make a whole series. Apply a thin coat of 'two pack' varnish to the front of the jar and position some carrot foliage and gypsophila (baby's breath) to form the outline.

Complete the floral design with some grass and a verbena flower. When the first coat of varnish is dry, apply a second coat, over the design, feathering the edges of the varnish with a lint-free cloth.

Cut a circle from white sticky-back plastic to fit the top of the lid. Repeat the floral design on the plastic, fixing the plants with latex adhesive. Cover the design with protective film and fix the circle to the lid. For that finishing touch, add a band of broderie anglaise around the lid.

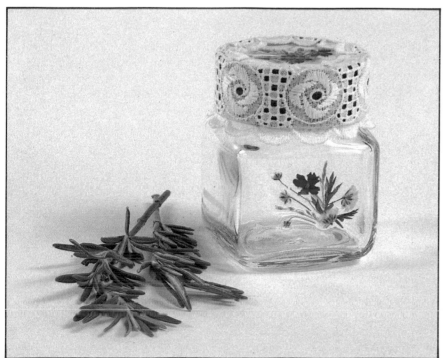

This solid perfume is simple to make, and looks so pretty in a matching green ceramic jar: a perfect complement to any dressing table. Begin creating the floral design on the insert card supplied with the lid. Fix three variegated geranium leaves in a triangular shape using latex adhesive.

Follow this outline with silverweed, yellow medick and two wood avens (clove root) flowers. Complete with a large wood avens flower at the base. Reassemble the lid.

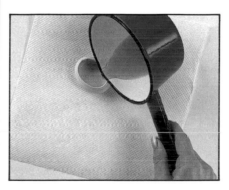

To make the perfume you will need 3 tsp of shredded beeswax, 2 tsp of almond oil, 15 drops of your chosen concentrated perfume oil and a drop of sap-green dye. Slowly melt the wax and almond oil over a very low heat. Remove the pan from the heat and, when the mixture has cooled a little, add the perfume and colour and pour it into the trinket box. It will then set hard and be ready for use.

Agold pendant makes a delightful setting for a delicate cream and brown design. Cut an oval of brown cardboard to fit, then select small cream buds and flowers of traveller's joy and hawthorn, and sprays of autumn coloured *Acaena microphylla* leaves. Form a soft crescent of leaves, placing dots of adhesive directly on to the card and teasing each leaf into place with a paintbrush.

Now add buds of traveller's joy and sprays of *Acaena* to complete the full crescent shape, using a toothpick to place the adhesive directly on to the back of the larger flowers.

Place a large hawthorn flower at the base of the design and highlight it by tucking flowers of traveller's joy under the petals. Fill in the crescent with the remaining smaller hawthorn flowers. Reassemble the pendant, taking care that when it is sealed the design card is packed tight under the glass.

This exquisite piece of matching jewellery simply needs a little patience to complete. Cut a white cardboard oval to fit the brooch and fix sprays of miniature maidenhair fern to create an outline. Scatter gypsophila (baby's breath) buds amongst the foliage, then add a cluster of red alyssum in the centre and a few blue forget-me-nots.

Now cut a white oval to fit the pendant. With the aid of toothpicks, fix two sprays of shepherd's purse foliage to the top and right of the card. Arrange flower stems to resemble the stems of a bunch of flowers. Now add curving gypsophila buds throughout the design.

Add buds of spiraea and shepherd's purse next, teasing them into place, over dots of adhesive, with a soft paintbrush. Use an open flower of red alyssum to form the focal point and bring some spiraea through the design from the left to the centre. Assemble the jewellery according to the manufacturer's instructions.

Make this delightful brooch from scratch! With a hacksaw cut a rectangle of thin mahogany 50mm by 75mm (2in by 3in). Round off the corners, front and back, with sandpaper. Give the brooch one thin coat of varnish and when completely dry, sand and varnish it again.

Form an outline on the sticky varnish with leaves of rock geranium, meadowsweet and common bent grass. Across this outline create a curving line of hawthorn flowers, tucking a few more leaves of rock geranium beneath the flowers as you go.

When the design is complete, coat with two or three layers of varnish, allowing each coat to dry in between applications. Finally, attach a brooch pin to the back of the wood with 'super' strong adhesive.

Many Victorian lockets or brooches were designed to take mementoes. This type of brooch is ideal for a miniature display of flowers. Cut a backing card to fit the brooch and cover it with foam. Now cut a larger oval from ivory silk and cover the foam with this. Make little snips into the overlapping edges of the silk as shown, wrap the edges round the backing card and glue down.

With latex adhesive fix a tip of frosted cow parsley leaf in the centre of the oval. At the top add pale peach candytuft and a wisp of common bent grass. Place more grass down the side of the design.

Add peach bistort to the left and red flowers of the spiraea 'Anthony Waterer' to the right and foreground. Finally, place an open flower of candytuft in the centre to form the focal point. Seal the design into the brooch using either the original backing or, if this is missing, packing it into an oval of thick cardboard.

INDEX

ACKNOWLEDGEMENTS

The publishers would like to thank the following for their
help in compiling this book:

Longmans Ltd. Florist, 46 Holborn Viaduct, London EC1,
(for making the wedding bouquet on page 71).

Framecraft Miniatures Ltd., 148-150 High Street, Aston, Birmingham.
Coca-Cola Great Britain, Pemberton House, Wrights Lane, London W8
The Covent Garden General Store, Long Acre, London WC2
David Mellor, St James Street, London WC2
Table Props Hire Ltd, Duncan Terrace, London N1

SUPPLIERS

Swan House Gallery, Ashfield, Stowmarket, Suffolk, England.
(Shop and mail order service run by author Mary Lawrence, specialized in the sale of pressed
flower accessories and designs, including presses, mounts, frames and wooden kits plus a
wide range of other items for displaying craftwork).

Mail order suppliers of items designed to display craftwork (such as porcelain
and crystal boxes, plaques, paperweights, fingerplates and napkin rings):

Framecraft Miniatures Ltd., 148-150 High Street, Aston, Birmingham, UK.
(supplying UK and Europe)

Anne Brinkley Designs, 21 Ransom Road, Newton Centre, Mass. 02159, USA.

Needlecraft International Pty. Ltd., 19 Railway Parade, Eastwood, NSW 2122, Australia.

Mrs Greville Parker, 286 Queen Street, Masterton, New Zealand.